Power and Morality in a Business Society

Power and Morality in a Business Society

Sylvia Kopald Selekman
*Former Fellow, Social Science
Research Council*

Benjamin M. Selekman
*Kirstein Professor of Labor
Relations, Harvard Graduate
School of Business Administration
Harvard University*

6421

McGRAW-HILL BOOK COMPANY, INC.
New York   Toronto   London

in memory of

Joseph L. Snider

esteemed colleague, who as a
searcher for moral meaning
stimulated this exploration

Preface

The social and moral responsibilities of industry have become a major concern of American businessmen during the past quarter of a century. It is a heartening development, yet one cannot help but be uneasy about what appear to be naive assumptions regarding the underlying factors which have evoked the concern.

For it is not failure in ordinary, decent, day-to-day human relationships but a moral crisis that confronts business as it does the rest of the community. We may take for granted that most businessmen are genuinely interested in the welfare of their employees and fellow citizens. The day of exploited and sweated labor is over, just as caveat emptor is pretty much a matter of history. Rare indeed is the businessman who has not learned by this time that in the long run his success is intertwined with the well-being and prosperity of both workers and customers.

The crisis which has led to the concern about social responsibility is much more complex. It stems from nothing less than the age-old problem of power—with its dangerous as well as its beneficent aspects. Not until businessmen recognize that they are the administrators of power systems can they face realistically the task of how to discharge morally the power they wield. In this day and age, social and moral imperatives carry with them not the giving up of material things but the giving up of absolute, unilateral power.

The moral involvement of power calls, in other words, for a new look at management and its authority. It means doing things *with* people as equals, not *for* them as inferiors. It means, indeed, that other power systems must be recognized and accepted—whether they be the power systems of labor, the state, the farmer, or other interest groups. And it means that businessmen must learn how to negotiate *with* others as equals, rather than dictate *to* them as subordinates.

But at the same time businessmen must hold on to power so as to safeguard the efficiency of their establishments; for without power it is impossible to operate effectively. And so a dilemma constantly faces businessmen as custodians and organizers of power and as negotiators with other power systems. Without full recognition of this dilemma and its complexities, all discussion about business responsibility takes on the nature of homilectics. Sermonizing does some good, but not much.

This essay is an attempt to explore the nature of this dilemma—the problems of power and morality: how power can be invested with moral purpose and at the same time be safeguarded for the work that must be done both for the particular institution and for the community as a whole.

For reading the manuscript and making helpful comments, thanks are due: Clinton S. Golden, Dr. A. Howard Myers, Merlyn S. Pitzele, Professors Raphael Demos, E. Robert Livernash, James J. Healy, and Stephen H. Fuller, Andrew R. Towl, Ruth C. Hetherston, Dean Donald K. David and Dean Stanley F. Teele; for illuminating editorial assistance, Robert Hutchinson of the McGraw-Hill Book Company; for seeing the book through the press and all attendant chores, my secretary, Selena Gardner.

The literature on the subject is vast, and only a few books can here be mentioned: *American Capitalism: The Concept of Countervailing Power* by John Kenneth Galbraith; *World Politics and Personal Insecurity* by Harold D. Lasswell;

Power and Society: A Framework for Political Inquiry by Harold D. Lasswell and Abraham Kaplan; *Political Power* by Charles E. Merriam; *Power and Conscience* by T. V. Smith; *Power: A New Social Analysis* by Bertrand Russell; *On Power: Its Nature and the History of Its Growth* by Bertrand de Jouvenel; *Goals of Economic Life* edited by A. Dudley Ward for the Study Committee of the Federal Council of the Churches of Christ in America; *In Defense of the National Interest* and *Politics Among Nations* by Hans J. Morgenthau; and *The Myth of the State* by Ernst Cassirer.

If any one person were to be singled out for his influence on our thinking, it would be the late John R. Commons and, particularly, three of his works, *The Legal Foundations of Capitalism, Institutional Economics: Its Place in Political Economy*, and *The Economics of Collective Action*.

Benjamin M. Selekman

Contents

part one

THE TECHNICAL "MUST"
VERSUS THE
ETHICAL "OUGHT"

1. *Power: liberator or enslaver?*

It is a lifetime of exposure to the impact of power on human relationships which has led us to undertake this exploration into power and morality. For both of us have seen and felt power from childhood on not only in the usual daily disciplines experienced as one grows up but also in the much harsher forms resorted to in the struggle shaking the social structure of the communities and the times in which we lived.

Power and human exploitation at beginning of century

One of us grew up, for instance, amidst coal and steel in western Pennsylvania. Here, during the first two decades of this century, I was a witness to the intermittent battles between miners and steelworkers on the one hand and their employers on the other over the right to have any voice in the conditions of work and life. And literally it was *life*, for in those days most of the miners not only worked in the pits of the employing companies but also lived in the company towns and bought all their provisions, clothing, and other necessities in the company stores. Rent and store bills were automatically deducted from earnings on pay day.

The strikes of those times were violent—invariably accompanied with damage to property, personal injury, and loss of life. The workers resorted to the use of naked power when picketing; the employers resorted to naked power when importing strikebreakers. These strikebreakers enjoyed the protection of private police such as Baldwin Fels' detectives and specially deputized sheriffs. The state constabulary, nominally neutral in their duty to maintain the peace, usually ended up in any particular strike by protecting property and strikebreakers. During one strike, I saw the brutal dispersal by the state constabulary of men, women, and children assembled on the main street of the town to hear a union organizer. The method was a simple one. The constabulary put spurs to their trained horses at the head of the street and rode through the crowd six abreast swinging their maces until most of their victims fell dazed or unconscious to the cobblestones. Those who escaped the horses' hoofs and the policemen's clubs scattered to the four winds.

During my last year in high school, I was so shocked at such brutal denial of the basic liberty of free assemblage—which I had been studying in my civics course—that I devoted my graduation oration to berating those in power, dragging in "Wall Street," of course, as well as "economic determinism" and "capitalistic imperialism"! The respectable townspeople blamed the school superintendent for permitting such a "subversive" speech to be made. They also snubbed me as I went

on my wonted errands to the grocer, the butcher, and the land-
lord, though I had been an erstwhile hero and a source of pride
because I was planning to go to college (something very few
from industrial towns did in those days).

Similarly, both of us witnessed the degradation of the sweat-
shops in the large cities—my late wife as she grew up in New
York, and I as from time to time I visited friends who held jobs
in the needle trades. Several of our friends became exhausted
under the harsh conditions prevailing in those unsanitary,
makeshift shops. Some became invalids with chronic illness.
A few died prematurely. Most of them were active participants
in building unions which were destined, after many strikes and
much violence, not only to eliminate so miserable a working
environment but also to collaborate with management in pio-
neering in such progressive measures as housing, banking,
workers' education, and arbitration machinery. Having witnessed, as young people, the degradation of workers, both of us
rejoiced when as grownups we were given an opportunity to
participate in these new forms of self-government, particularly
in workers' education and in arbitration.

On my first job, I again witnessed a power struggle. I was
assigned to make a field study of the aftermath of the bitter
and violent strike which the miners had waged for fifteen
months in 1913 and 1914 against the Colorado Fuel and Iron
Company in Huerfano and Las Animas counties. In one of the
battles between striking miners and militia at Ludlow, eleven
children and two women had been smothered to death when the
tents in which they lived after eviction from company houses
were ignited by flying bullets exchanged between miners and
soldiers. In addition, I observed events and interviewed the
steelworkers of the same company at the Pueblo works as they

participated, almost to a man, in the nation-wide steel strike in 1919.

Fortunately, I was to observe in Colorado not only the impact of economic and political power, with all its grim manifestation in naked violence, but also the influence of moral power. For John D. Rockefeller had been shocked and stung into action by the exposure of President Wilson's Industrial Relations Commission of what went on in a company which his family controlled. With the help of Clarence Hicks, recruited from the YMCA movement, and W. L. Mackenzie King, then ex-deputy Minister of Labor and later Prime Minister of Canada, he drafted a plan of employee representation, known in time as the Rockefeller Plan. It aimed to give the miners and the steelworkers a vehicle for voicing their grievances, as well as for participating in determining wages and working conditions. So dedicated was Rockefeller in his moral purpose that he personally visited the working communities in Colorado–not without risk–and himself explained to the miners the intent and purpose of his plan.

Power and human emancipation by mid-century

One could go on at length portraying the human suffering and maladjustments arising out of clashes of power in industry in those early years. But it is better to draw the curtain on that scene and lift it again approximately a quarter of a century later. We see now a complete and dramatic change. The unions representing steelworkers, coal miners, clothing, and garmentworkers are now fully established and recognized. Their legitimacy, like that of all organized labor, is now explicitly sanctioned by law and upheld by the vigorous administration of a Federal agency. The miners, the steelworkers, the tailors, enjoy not only the highest wages in the world (real wages, not just money wages!) but also holidays and vacations with pay, pensions, sickness and hospital benefits, and, well on the way, assured minimum earnings when laid off. In the communities where they live, they and their unions now occupy an important and, not infrequently, a dominant position. In the affairs of their respective industries, the unions exercise a potent voice, heard with respect and sometimes with misgiving by management. For in the eyes of the latter—by this time a professionally trained corps of men as compared with the hardboiled superintendent and foreman of a generation ago—the constant pressure for wage increases, greater benefits, and an ever wider "say" in industry may imperil the capacity of business to function efficiently; the whole economy, indeed, may be upset by these pressures. With the threats of inflation or rigidities in costs, business may find it difficult to keep competitive and to plan and develop new enterprises—a necessity for the economic growth and prosperity of the nation.

It is not our purpose here to examine the pros and cons in the positions of unions or corporations, but, rather, to etch with a few broad strokes the contrast between the 1950s and the situation as it prevailed before the 1930s. For economic and political power—reinforced by moral power—has brought about a complete change during our lifetime in the social and economic structure of the nation. The acceleration of scientific power, moreover, during two world wars has laid the basis not only for great material wealth and strength but also for the nightmare vision of the destruction of the civilization which the same scientific power has helped to preserve and foster.

And, just as both of us were witnesses to the unsocial exploitation of power in the early years of this century, so have we been privileged to witness and to participate as teachers, researchers, consultants, and arbitrators, in the socializing of power in the past quarter century.

But power was seen by one of us in still another phase. My wife grew up under the influence of Daniel De Leon's Socialist Labor Party, a form of socialism more akin to the Russian Marxism of Lenin than to the American socialism of Debs or Thomas. At first, she rejoiced when the Czars were displaced by the Bolsheviks. But the joy was destined to prove short-lived. She recoiled with distaste and disillusionment as Lenin, and later Stalin, imposed a massive slavery upon the Russian people, a slavery soon to be copied by Mussolini and Hitler as they merged collectivism and nationalism into fascism and Nazism as a façade for completely subjugating and brutalizing their peoples. What a contrast America offered as it grappled with its problems from day to day to emerge into the humanitarian nation of the 1950s.

Indeed, anyone who has lived through the first half of this century in this country cannot help being impressed with the changed and changing status of women, of minorities, of wage earners. To be sure, the movement for greater freedom has been an uneven one, particularly in the matter of equality for racial and ethnic minorities. Nevertheless, in contrast with the enslavement of whole peoples by Nazism, fascism, and communism, the period in the United States amounts to one of liberation. There is even a contrast, not so sharp to be sure, between events in this country and the nations of Western Europe, from whom we inherited the great basic liberties of mankind. The contrast is not between freedom and enslavement, but rather between the vitality of the American people and in Europe a sort of dead-center standstill—even perhaps timidity—in carrying out an early promise for the liberation of man.

American power and human freedom on global scale

We do not intend to pause and examine the probable causes of these striking differences between this country and Europe. Two world wars constitute an obvious factor; for in Eastern and Central Europe the aftermath in misery and destruction enabled ruthless men with fixed ideologies to seize power and, under the guise of collectivism, mislead and subjugate their demoralized and disillusioned fellow nationalists. The same wars exhausted France and Great Britain. For over a year, indeed, Britain stood alone in the breach in a life-and-death struggle against evil tyranny.

We entered both wars, but we entered them late. Our allies were well-nigh exhausted before we fully awoke to the peril of a victory for the forces of tyranny. Our power, in spite of its tardy mobilization, turned the scales. But instead of finding ourselves exhausted, we emerged with our strength augmented to greater heights than it had ever known before. Indeed, both times we came out as the strongest nation of the globe. We withdrew from the world scene after World War I. In retrospect, our withdrawal constituted an abdication of responsibility, but this is not to say that, even had we stayed in, World War II would have been prevented. For Nazism and fascism were new forms of tyranny. It is questionable whether we, any more than the British and French with their much greater experience in statecraft and diplomacy, would have had the wisdom to lead the free world so as to discourage the evil forces within Germany before Hitler could let loose upon the world the most horrible war ever waged.

After World War II, however, we did stay in with the rest of the civilized world, and the results, whatever the initial discouragement, have been most heartening. Without us, Russian

communism would no doubt by now be ensconced on the Eura-
sian continent, from the English Channel to the Pacific, with
still more satellites within her domain than she boasts of now.
For this time, sensing at last our self-interest, we not only
stayed with our friends but also assumed the responsibility of
leadership and, together with our allies, forged the North At-
lantic community, a power block strong enough to counterbal-
ance Russian power. And by means of the Marshall Plan
and other forms of assistance, we have helped the European
democracies gradually regain their spirit and their strength.
While we differ in many things, the Western community is becoming more an alliance of self-respecting and articulate nations. It now looks, indeed, as if Russia, checkmated as she is,
may seriously enter into negotiation with the West to work out
a possible pattern of coexistence.

Now what is impressive in all this is that power has constituted the primary factor in bringing about critical changes for
good or for evil. Our power proved decisive in winning two
world wars, and, as this is written, may be turning the scales
toward a workable peace—or at least a stalemate under which
Russia may rely on diplomacy and subversion, rather than
physical attack, to gain her ends. So long as a resort to raw
power is thus avoided and the tests shifted to the diplomatic
front, the hope remains strong that not only may destructive
war be prevented but also that we may have a more than
equal chance of winning the battle for men's minds.

Shifts of power and inevitable scapegoats

Within the national scene, too, power constituted the primary factor behind the movement for liberation. It was by
mobilizing their political power and making alliances with

liberal and reform groups that women gained their right to participate equally with men in government. Labor achieved its new status by unremittingly building its strength on the economic and political front. Progress in this instance was, it is true, retarded until the great depression of the thirties; and, in those prostrate days, many workers became as disillusioned as their European brethren. But it was our good fortune that the leaders of the incipient labor movement had not become discouraged by the rebuffs historically received at the hands of industry. For this was the time when Hitler and Mussolini rose to strength. It was the time when Stalin strengthened his vise on the Russian people. In our country, fortunately, more conservative labor leaders were followed, and in a short period of twenty years, we witnessed the growth of a powerful labor movement. Farmers also rose to new strength in the economic and political arena. Massive social and welfare legislation was enacted.

In the heat of the moment there were also negative outbursts, and attacks of one group upon another filled the air. Business became a convenient scapegoat; having been at the direction of the economic life of the nation for so long a period, it could hardly escape the searching, if unfriendly, criticism which followed. Nor could it escape the legislation enacted to regulate its activities and minimize the abuses, real or fancied, which the people thought had brought about the great depression. Thus again the century was shaken by a shift in power.

Nature of power

Power shifts such as these have long been the subject of study and observation. What has not been adequately studied, however—and what we must consider if we are to understand the time in which we live—is the nature of power itself: power as liberator and creator; power as enslaver and destroyer. By power we mean all the essential phases of energy which help to free man from backbreaking drudgery and thus make his life actually and potentially more productive and creative. But we must hasten to add that power also includes those phases of energy which threaten man with servitude and, in its latest form, with destruction. To be more specific, by power we mean the power of nature uncovered by science; the power of man as he organizes himself and his fellow men through a multiplicity of economic and political activities and institutions to do better cooperatively (and competitively) what he cannot do by himself; and finally, the power of morality—the body of religious and ethical doctrines which every man socially inherits, and which thus, in the American ethos, shapes men's ideals toward the kind of society envisioned by the Judaic-Christian and the Greco-Roman traditions.

The challenge of deploying power creatively

We stand, thus, in the middle of the twentieth century with new groups in positions of great power within the nation, and, as a nation among nations, with a vitality that has been paralleled only in a few periods of history. One would think that, with this peak strength, America would be secure, sure of itself, ready to move forward. A malaise, however, seems to be besetting us. We are unsure of ourselves. We are sensitive to criticism. We are misunderstood. We find that people elsewhere are not happy with our leadership. Even our generosity is turned against us. Internally, we are ill at ease and suspicious of one another—so much so that at times we seem in danger of forgetting our fundamental belief in the dignity of man.

We enjoy a standard of living unparalleled in the world or in all history; but we do not enjoy life. We are mobile in our cars and see the whole world in television. Yet we are not sure where we want to go or what we want to see. Our very power baffles us, and we do not know how to turn it into creative expression both as a nation and as individual citizens. We recoil from the charge of materialism and the challenge that a system based on private enterprise can never achieve a moral life. And so we answer defensively. We deny. We scold. Sometimes we are tempted to withdraw—and, indeed, threaten with "agonizing reappraisals." We suffer from a gnawing sense of guilt and sin and from a lack of confidence and mutual trust. Most of all, incredible as it may seem, America is afraid. Indeed at times it seems as if the most powerful people on the face of the earth are suffering from one of the worst cases of jitters known.

Such a situation, if continued, is in danger of eventually sapping our vitality. Unless we try to understand the fundamental nature of our society as interrelated systems of power—scientific, business, political, and moral—we are in danger of failing in our mission, the mission to establish a great civilization on this continent and to lead the way toward peace and security for mankind.

This book we hope is a modest contribution toward this end. America's power has made her fearful all the more because its dimension is so great. For as a people we hesitate to accept the fact that power is an essential for progress and freedom. We are haunted by the age-old suspicion that power is evil, as indeed it is, unless it is checked, contained, and directed. How may such an objective be attained and how can the objective be worked out in day-to-day living—the objective of diminishing the evil and enhancing the beneficent aspects of power? To what extent does our history demonstrate that such an objective is attainable? What light do reason and human association throw on the all-important task of taming power? Similarly, what administrative and integrating activity, natural to our national way of doing things, is available as a stabilizer and director of power?

We have deliberately avoided in this book the heavy apparatus of scholarship. Thus we have not tried to be "taxonomic," that is, to define the various kinds of power or to classify them. We may even at times have oversimplified matters, but not, we hope, at the expense of truth or making clear the vast difficulties which confront us.

The fulfillment of man's aspirations for effective and moral living is, and must be, a never ending quest. What we wish above all is to get our fellow Americans excited about the great opportunity which has come to them because of the vast power they have inherited and developed—not to fear it or apologize for it, but, rather, to deploy it in a way to enrich and ennoble us and the rest of the world.

2. *The dilemma of power*

One of the paradoxes of the mid-twentieth century surely to be noted by future historians has been a recurrent warning against *fear* addressed to Americans—citizens of the most powerful, and one would think most serene, nation of the time. Thus, we are urged by President Eisenhower, as we were a quarter of a century ago by President Roosevelt, "to cleanse our hearts and minds of fear." We are beset by fear: we fear the atomic arsenal and the hydrogen bomb; we fear the men in the Kremlin; we fear subversion, treason, and sabotage; we fear business, labor, and government. Like primitive man, we fear certain words and phrases, certain ideas as though they had power in themselves. And we fear, too, the erosion of our freedoms under pressure to conform.

Yet, paradoxically enough, we have achieved at the same time a position of power beyond anything ever realized before by any other nation. Indeed, though the most confident of nations from the beginning, we seem in recent years sorely shaken and uncertain at the very time of peak power.

How does such formidable power exist side by side with multiplying, intensifying fears? Perhaps we must reexamine the very nature of power itself to understand how to gain mastery over our own fears and confusions.

Indeed, it may be that we shall find that it is the very possession of power that causes the fear and confusion which beset us. In a Judaic-Christian environment, power always begets a sense of sin and guilt. Power pricks the conscience of moral responsibility. Power awakens a sense of stewardship. Is America, as our detractors say, primarily a godless, materialistic nation? Are businessmen exploiters of men and of resources for private profit only? Indeed, is profit itself a sufficient measure of progress? Again, are we projecting a new form of imperialism among the peoples of the world? In brief, is our power bound, unless countervailing forces are launched against us, to corrupt us as it has so many peoples before?

The shape of power in modern America differs in more than one detail from that in other nations. The outstanding contrast lies indubitably in the focal role still played by private business in the conduct of our affairs. Most other institutions found in America are shared by men the world over. Science and technology are cultivated universally. Democracy in variant forms has long been established in Western nations, as have religious and moral codes. Only business, the motor to our industrial power, is uniquely American.

The moral isolation of American business

The suspicion directed against American business as an accepted mode of organizing economic life appears even more striking when viewed against the backdrop of history. The Industrial Revolution was first carried forward in England under the aegis of private enterprise. Most nations which undertook industrialization later made corporate business a major instrument of economic advance. Today, however, underdeveloped nations embarking upon industrialization do not resort primarily to private enterprise. Instead, direction is furnished by the state through controlled and closely directed government corporations. Even in the Free West of Europe, government controls have gone far in transforming the patterns of administering the national economy. Private enterprise gives way everywhere before the advancing welfare state. The United States, despite its mildly regulated economy, stands forth as the last stronghold of corporate management.

This isolation from the world of nations has had a psychological impact on our citizens difficult to measure. We are subjected not only to the attacks of rival social systems, the misrepresentations of foes, and the criticism of friends but also to deep uncertainties within our own midst—uncertainties in particular as to whether, despite our material success, our system results in justice both within the nation and in our dealings with other nations.

Uncertainties surround our business economy despite accomplishments

And just as our anxiety has increased with our peak powers, so the uncertainties still surrounding our business economy have coincided with a record of outstanding accomplishment. The years of the great depression marked, it is true, a sharp collapse of confidence in business leadership. It was not the first time, certainly, that businessmen had been the targets for attack and hostility. But never before had they suffered such widespread criticism as during those unhappy days.

Thus it was that the first rallying cry against fear sounded by President Roosevelt, "We have nothing to fear but fear itself," evoked different reactions from those called forth some two decades later by President Eisenhower's "We could not live in fear of each other forever." In 1933 it was the state of our economy that gave rise to our predominant anxieties. The Federal government came to the assistance of private enterprise with shoring-up and rescue operations. But, when the depression was over and reappraisal began, the old positions of business were never completely recaptured. With the rise of Nazism and fascism abroad and with government controls under war influence at home, fear shifted to the state, as men observed everywhere the drift from local to central government. At the same time, the groups that were assisted by government proved unwilling to relinquish the props that Washington had furnished them. In so far as reaffirmations in free enterprise were again sounded, they had the hollow ring of a booster's propaganda. At best they based their case upon potential threats to *freedom*, which are implicit in government regulation and control. And they had little effect in changing the dominant attitude of the times. Business, as an institutional network for administering the economy, remained on probation—not only abroad but also with a large element of our own people.

It is important to reckon soberly with this grudging acceptance of private business. It underlines one of the confused strands in the evolving American dilemma. For, if our fears exist in the midst of undeniable power, our doubts regarding corporate management coexist with equally undeniable accomplishments in the industrial world. The intrinsic strength of the American economy was sharply tested and proved, not only by the crisis of stagnation which affected the whole globe in the 1930s, but also by the demands of world war, reconstruction abroad, and renewed defense and war. It is not enough to credit war and postwar shortages as the major stimulus to full production. For other nations simultaneously faced the same demands of war and postwar reconstruction. But only the American economy proved itself able to turn out arms *and* butter, to serve as the major arsenal for the Western alliance, to help its allies rehabilitate themselves after the war, *and*, at the same time, to facilitate a historic rise in the living standards of its people.

Granting differences between our opportunity and that of other nations—our vast resources, our large internal market, our distance from theatres of war—nevertheless the fact remains that we have been neither weak nor niggardly in using our wealth for human defense and human progress. To be sure, no one group can claim sole credit for our accomplishment. Nevertheless, since business management has been directing our industrial establishment, at the least it deserves credit for having discharged efficiently a mandate to turn out guns and butter.

Why, then, have such tangible accomplishments failed to dispel the doubts of the American people? Why have unmatched national powers failed to lift the pall of fear? The presence of uncertainty in the midst of business accomplishment is as paradoxical as that of fear in the midst of national power. The related paradoxes indeed reinforce one another to

point up the underlying profound dilemma of which they are
part.

Contemporary situation as moral crisis

In truth, the dilemma is not that of government or business
alone, but is a more profound one involving both. It is a *moral*
problem facing man in all his relationships. The age-old conflict between good and evil has emerged in portentous modern
shape, grown more frightful by the destructive potential locked
in the new instruments of global war and similarly by the vast
power, economic, political, and technological, now within the
control of the rulers of men. Thus it is that present-day philoso-
phers of history and religion are searching for spiritual and
religious reaffirmations which will restore man to the dignity
of his human estate.

The problem is not as simple as it appears. On the one hand,
old questions concerning the justification of production for
profit have never been resolved. Thus everywhere, at home
and abroad, spokesmen for labor have added to the older shib-
boleth of human rights versus property rights, the rights of men
to secure not only well-paid and regular employment but also
the amenities of life–holidays, vacation, and insurance of all
sorts, whether provided by business or government or both. On
the other hand, our business society seems to face in ever dis-
proportionate measure–perhaps because of our very power in
the world–the latter-day universal moral challenge of spiritual
and aesthetic values in an industrial age booming with material
success. Thus man, who has always been a problem to himself,
actually has within his grasp, for the first time, the power to

control his society. But since he knows power primarily as an antisocial force he finds himself at once king and pawn of the world.

America haunted by ethical challenge

But to repeat these traditional challenges is not to resurrect the musty odor of stale debate but rather to face another paradox. For, in matters of social responsibility, mid-century America is not found wanting. Americans certainly enjoy standards of living and security higher than any other people, and higher than any ever known before. Whatever may have been the comparable record in the past, certainly within the last quarter century, which marks our transition to world leadership, the United States has kept in the forefront of revisions in moral responsibility too.

Nor has America been found wanting in trying to share the burdens of other nations in the tasks of reconstruction and peace. It gave up a century of isolationism. It extended material help—through the Marshall Plan, Economic Cooperation, and Point Four—in a way unknown and unexpected in past history. To be sure, the role of a great national power in a technologically shrinking world entails reassessments of cultural ways and fundamental revisions of policy—foreign as well as domestic. We need not claim what no other people can claim: a completely satisfactory answer to the moral revaluations of men's responsibilities for their fellows whether abroad or at home. But it is a heartening strand in our changing destiny that the twentieth century must register the last business economy in the front ranks of those who face up to, and hope to make headway against, this moral crisis of power engulfing us all.

The dilemma of power

Why then, with such a record, do we feel so uncertain, so unsure of ourselves?

Quite naturally we see the contemporary moral dilemma first and primarily in American terms. Yet the component elements of the crisis represent a universal experience. For the dilemma of power is intrinsic for every people whether pre-industrial, industrializing, or industrialized. It is in the handling of the dilemma that national diversity leaves its impress. In order to handle it now, Americans will need certainly to understand the nature of the powers that science and technology in a highly developed industrial society have placed at their command. They will need to know the challenges and the dangers confronting them as compared to those confronting industrial man elsewhere. They will need to know as well the checks and curbs their heritage has made available for directing power toward ends deemed good, and how decisions on the use of power are made, tested, carried forward, and revised.

What they must realize is that these powers are constantly changing. If private enterprise remains the outstanding mobilizer of productive power, it is hardly today what it was a century ago. As a matter of fact, with the rise of union labor and state regulation, the power of businessmen has declined relatively in the United States. Moreover, mere changes in ownership do not solve old problems. They indeed may create far thornier new ones. Certainly no one can henceforth rely upon the transformations of corporate ownership as the answer to the moral dilemma of power that Marxian theory envisaged. In domestic affairs, quite as much as in international affairs, "power abhors a vacuum." The state that replaces the owning classes neither withers away nor enthrones the proletariat. The politician instead becomes king. And the combination of political, economic, and technological power gives him an absolute power over subjects who are no longer truly free citizens with a voice in their own destiny.

Power an essential of social life

There is a deceptive simplicity in defining the moral crisis in which we are caught as basically a dilemma of power. Throughout recorded history men have become familiar with the perils of power. Power has traditionally been weighted in the direction of evil, as a danger against which we must remain eternally vigilant. Certainly the propensity for absolutism and evil in power exercised by some men over other men remains part of the problem—and in our day of crisis a particularly thorny part. But it is not the whole dilemma, for we are confronted from the outset with the fact that power constitutes an *essential* of human life in society. The notion, shocking as it may be at first hearing, that society cannot dispense with power must, indeed, be accepted as an essential premise for practical understanding of the problems created by it and for a way of handling them. For power is no more and no less than those energies of forces harnessed to human capacity as a way of rendering more effective man's activities in the promotion of his purposes.

The main categories of powers: (1) *scientific,* (2) *economic,* (3) *political, and* (4) *moral*

Moreover, power is not only an inescapable prerequisite of effective performance, but it is also a diverse one. The very tensions of present-day discussions prepare us for such diversity. We have for some time now been engaged in an endless drumfire of debate about the implications of atomic power, industrial power, military power, agrarian power, business power, labor power, regional power, and so on.

For the purposes of the exploration we are undertaking in this book, all these various powers are classed into four main categories: (1) scientific and technological; (2) economic; (3) political; and (4) moral. Obviously, these boundaries are indicated only for purposes of analysis. In the untidy realities of everyday living, these powers overlap and interweave. The work of men in the laboratories of science are interconnected constantly with those who manage business undertakings in the offices and the mills of industry, or with those in the councils of politics which affect them all. And, all the while, our common moral values remain part of each human being's equipment, as well as being the stuff and substance of every context in which human activity takes place.

In other words, the activities encompassed within the four categories of power are ultimately integrated or combined to carry forward the production of wealth and services deemed necessary to modern society. Yet in studying power and its uses, one must recognize that the four categories of power— scientific, economic, political and ethical—are at the same time separate and distinctive. They are set into motion by the characteristic daily activities of men with special skills and training, often with specialized equipment, in particular factories, business offices, government centers, laboratories, universities, and churches. Performance is measured as good or effective in terms of the criteria explicit in science and implicit in business, politics, education, and religion. The powers are mobilized, moreover, to be used.

The very nature of a specialized society such as ours, however, creates a perplexing situation, for the men who mobilize many of these powers—particularly in science and technology and frequently in business—are not necessarily the same as those who decide the uses to which the powers are to be put and the goals to which the powers are to be harnessed—or even *how* these powers are to be utilized in moving toward those goals. Today more than at any other time in history, the separation of those who make power from those who direct the use of the power created gives rise to the major perplexity at the heart of the contemporary moral crisis—and may help to explain how both fear and strength may come from the possession of power.

Beyond this perplexity is the conflict, as we shall presently see, between the amoral, or ethically neutral, values in power as power inherent in science, politics, and industry, and the *ethical* values of the Judaic-Christian morality inherited by men as the administrators of power—the basic, perversive conflict between a technical "must" and an ethical "ought."

The problem then becomes: How can we prevent power, amoral in the main as it is in its genesis, from becoming destructive and antisocial? What we must discover is whether power, which strikes fear into the heart of man, can be tamed and directed towards creative, social purposes.

3. *Ethical neutrality and*

moral involvement in power

It is the fact that power as a technical entity—as organized force or energy—is, with the exception of moral power, amoral or ethically neutral, that gives rise to the moral dilemma of power. In fact, (it is this *separation* of the technical powers from moral power that is intrinsic in the dilemma of the businessman and, for that matter, of all other administrators who find it necessary to use power with, and over, men in carrying out their respective jobs.) For man is not only the creator of power, the decision-maker on goals toward which it is to be used, and the actual administrator of power, but he is also the carrier of moral values. He is thus deeply and constantly involved in the ethical implications of the uses to which power is put.

Technical powers and varying moral involvement

The degree of involvement, however, in this conflict between technical and moral values varies. The scientist as scientist is least involved. Presumably he is completely absorbed in the technical demands of his work. He may well be a dedicated man in search of truth and, as such, be motivated by the highest values in every step he takes in his laboratory. But, as his project develops, his materials, methods of work, and results are viewed both by himself as well as by the large community impersonally–that is to say, apart from human consequences. The power he releases may indeed be used for war or peace; for construction or destruction. Thus, his activities as a scientist are the most ethically neutral of the activities of all those engaged in making essential power available for society.

As a citizen, the scientist may, of course, have grave misgivings as to the consequences of his discoveries for society, as witness Dr. Oppenheimer's brooding on whether we should proceed with the development of the hydrogen bomb. The position of the community as interpreted by the Federal government was that, as citizen Dr. Oppenheimer was within his rights; but as scientist entrusted with leadership in developing nuclear weapons–well, that was another question. His very reluctance to proceed seemed to disqualify him, and, then, tragically enough, question as to security arose. His past was delved into again, though he had been cleared to serve as director of Los Alamos. Thus all sorts of moral issues became confused; and who of us rests with an easy conscience about Oppenheimer's "dismissal" from the assignment in which he had proved himself so competent? But Dr. Oppenheimer in yielding to the moral dictates of his conscience in a sense precipitated the crisis himself when he stepped out of his role as scientist into that of policy maker on the use of the power to be developed. In the cold war between East and West it was for others to decide whether the bomb should be made as a deterrent. Dr. Oppenheimer's task as scientist was to help create this power entity.

The businessman, on the other hand, who organizes the economic power of industry, enjoys not even as much freedom from moral involvement as that of the scientist—precisely because intrinsic in his daily job is the constant making of decisions on the use of his power. In this process men are involved at every step, with frequently conflicting interests as investors, as managers, as employees, as competitors, and as consumers. Thus, business injects human—and, so, morally saturated —issues into the technical consideration as to how economic power is to be used.

If business may be said to be more morally involved than science, government as the exerciser of political power is more involved than either. For a businessman's ability to mobilize and wield power is dependent on the production of profit. To maintain profits, it is frequently necessary to pursue such policies as laying off people, moving plants, raising prices, and so forth, which, in the short run, at least—and not infrequently in the long run—may turn out to be harmful to some individuals and communities. The state, on the other hand, carries the greatest degree of human involvement, since its whole purpose is the protection and welfare of its citizens, from police and military functions to the administration of justice and provisions against the social hazards of living in an industrial community.

The state may be said, therefore, in theory at least, to be committed to the most moral of activities. But the state is an abstraction. In reality, political parties and individual office-holders actually exercise the power of government. In practice, politicians, in order to hold and perpetuate power, run the whole gamut of moral, amoral, and, at times, even immoral behavior. For political activity is the least rigorous of all human action in meeting technical criteria. The party seeking power frequently engages in irresponsible promises and performance, an irresponsibility which the scientist or businessman must avoid at greatest peril if he is to continue to enjoy confidence. Moreover, while science and industry encompass the wealth-producing activities, politics focuses primarily on the distribution of wealth. The "producers" must meet technical tests of actually making, pricing, and selling the goods; the "distributors" can play fast and loose. The power to tax and use public funds makes it easy to avoid standards of efficiency; costs, therefore, are often hidden and indirect.

The tests that scientists must meet of good work, work well done by the rules of scientific method in the judgment of their work peers, are again, much more rigorous than those confronting businessmen. The latter, however, must still answer to measurable tests of economic performance as evaluated in terms of costs, efficiency, and profits. Political organizations, on the other hand, bypass the tests applicable in science and business. Certainly government officials must exercise skills and meet criteria of effective work done, particularly in the permanent administrative agencies. But politics is intrinsically a matter of the getting and holding of office, and as such it is never separable from the men who seek power. It is from the outset a power of men, for men, over men. Emotionalism, manipulation, demagogy are always potential, as is the temptation to make easy promises no matter how difficult to fulfill. Accordingly, measurable technical standards applicable to its activities prove far more difficult. To be sure, business, too, frequently engages in questionable activity, such as distortion in advertising, misrepresentation, and so on. But business has no coercive power. In that area, the consumer is king. The state alone enjoys the greatest sovereignty and the most dangerous power—coercive power of duress, of imprisonment, and even of death.

Distinction between moral power and technical power

In contrast to the ethical neutrality of scientific, economic, and political power, moral power consists exclusively of values which weigh decisions in the direction of ethical goals. Indeed, at first blush, umbrage might be taken at the very designation of the term *power* to our most treasured sentiments—of virtue, justice, righteousness, and the like. And certainly it is true that in America the separation of church and state ensures that these sentiments cannot be imposed by law. Yet, the impact of moral consciousness is so compelling that its power constitutes a major check against exploiting scientific, economic, and political power for self-aggrandizement. For, though, in a physical sense, moral power is the least coercive of all power, man finds himself dominated by the imperatives of the codes by which he lives. Beginning with early childhood, he is impregnated with secular and religious ideals which haunt him day and night. Indeed, it is moral power that creates the constant tension in man between what he does and what he ought to do.

Two scales of evaluation: technical and moral

The nature of power, accordingly, ranges men's activities along two prime scales of evaluation: (1) technical "musts," intrinsic in the activities that mobilize the diverse but essential powers; and (2) the ethical "oughts," ranging from the greatest degree of ethical neutrality characteristic of science, through the intensifying impact of moral values upon business and politics, to the complete emphasis upon ethical goals in the moral system. Furthermore, since the human agent is always involved as executor of power, no power ever is completely divorced from a moral involvement. The power made available by science stirs us so profoundly precisely because its potential results stand forth so threatening and demonic in their implication for man, particularly when harnessed to political power. The power of science, which at the dawn of our nation we regarded as beneficent, and the power of centralized government, which we regarded as evil, loom now in combination as the most threatening to mankind; for in the destructive tools turned out by science and in the drift toward centralization in government, we sense once more the possibility of absolute evil which is potential in all power unless harnessed by a vigilant community for progressive human purposes.

Thus forces that were to liberate men—popular government and the scientific temper—now shadow him with new and unimaginable tyrannies, precisely by measure of the technical powers that government and science now command. At the same time, if we are to be realistic, we must continue to marshal these powers. And by the same token, if no class of power holders can be trusted with absolute authority to make final and binding decisions, the taming and the control of power emerge as the central challenge. We must examine, therefore, in more detail, not only the nature of the power systems, but also the way power can be tamed and turned toward constructive goals.

In pointing up the moral implications of the various categories of power, much that has been said so far has necessarily been oversimplified. We turn, therefore, to a fuller examination of each category of power—and the moral dilemma it presents.

4. *The power of science*

It is appropriate that we should begin with science and technology in our exploration of the moral dilemma of power. For science constitutes, at one and the same time, the wellspring of our material power and the locus of our thorniest moral problems.

We have traditionally looked to science to free us from want, from fear, from superstition; and, for the most part, it has done exactly that. Yet, recently, from its familiar features, a second face has shown itself in the demonic face of evil, threatening new fears—indeed, new cataclysms.

Science, though ethically neutral, precipitates moral crisis of power

Here, then, at the outset of our inquiry we are brought up against the very heart of the dilemma. As power, as a means of mobilizing nature's energy and enhancing man's capacities to act effectively, the force of modern science has been without parallel in historic experience. The American, who enjoys the highest living standard ever known, owes it primarily to the secrets and methods unlocked by the sciences, pure and applied. Yet the same science and technology that have proved so frequently beneficial have also given birth to A-bombs and H-bombs. At the same time, science has provided us with instruments of communication capable either of enlightening man about the world he lives in, or of holding his mind captive. Most of the time these powerful instruments confuse him by bringing to his door the endless and frequently frantic debate over containment and preventive war, over cold wars and hot, over subversion and disloyalty. Thus, if science is power, it is a normally neutral, amoral power, with potentialities for good or evil commensurate with the scope of its technical force.

The scale of modern science sharpens moral crisis

The dilemma of power in its modern form is brought even more sharply into focus by the grand scale of operations on which science and technology are now conducted. For, if we are to understand scientific power as it exists today, we must realize that it is no longer a matter of single laboratories and lone inventors working late into the night, but that it has emerged instead as large-scale, continuous, organized research, with findings and invention separated from use and application to life situations. Inventions and new tools have, to be sure, a long lineage, from the digging stick and plowshare to the steam shovel and tractor; from the abacus to electronic computers, guided missiles, and nuclear energy, through all the discoveries which fill the annals of history. To the early scientist, however, who began as an inventor and empirical craftsman, moral problems of discovery and use were not separate issues. But, by the latter part of the nineteenth century, the gap between discovery and use began to widen. With the world wars of the twentieth century, government entered into scientific activities, particularly in World War II, with large subsidies to industry and large-scale undertakings under its own auspices. Thus science has been transformed into a continuous major activity in American society.

With these recent developments, the web of technical performance and moral involvement seems to be closing in upon scientists. Although science is of all the powers least bound by ethical imperatives, technical *expertise*, as we have seen, cannot always insulate even the scientist from ethical involvement, as in the relatively simpler days before the bomb. Witness, again, the Oppenheimer episode, in which the leader of the team that developed the A-bomb was, a few years later, denied access to the files of the Atomic Energy Commission because he confessed to moral scruples about developing the H-bomb.

Relation of power of science to other power systems: business and government

The large-scale development of science coincides, moreover, with an acceleration of power in the other two power systems dominating modern life, namely, the economic power of business and the political power of government. The contemporary fear, therefore, is not a fear of science in itself, but a fear of science joined with industry, or science joined with government. Government, for example, in its defense program, supplies the billions required for the research, the elaborate facilities, the industrial contractors, the laboratory projects, the trained staffs; and, thus, government constitutes a major factor in the growing sector of continuing research, pure and applied. But government also constitutes a nexus of power—and a growing one—in industrial society. When science was in its infancy in the new American republic, the newly formed Federal government emerged limited and checkmated by a written constitution. Indeed, the explicit intention at that time was to cut government down to size, in contrast to feudal, mercantile, mother-country models. Today, with science itself a formidable power, one of the aspects of the time which gives great concern arises out of its subsidization and control by the Federal government and the augmented power thus accruing to central authority.

Of the 25.3 billion dollars expended for research and development in our nation from 1941 to 1952, over half was done by or for the government. But the significant facts are that the annual amounts increased enormously—from 0.9 billion to 3.75 billion—and that the government's share shifted from about 40 per cent to 60 per cent—or from 0.37 billion to over 2.2 billion. Furthermore, while the government's own performance of this work increased slightly—from 0.2 billion to 0.8 billion—the burden of the government's programs was increasingly borne by the diversion of the talent of American industrial research.[1] And most of the growth in government-financed research and development comes from an increasing emphasis on defense. Thus, while only 0.029 billion was expended for this purpose in 1940, it was estimated as this book was going to press that, out of the 4.5 billion projected for the nation as a whole in the year 1955–1956, government-financed work would take 2.4 billion, of which 2.05 billion would be allocated to defense.[2]

Nor is any easy alternative on the horizon. In the contempo-

[1] U.S. Department of Defense, *The Growth of Scientific Research and Development*, Resources Division Bulletin No. 114/34, July 27, 1953.

[2] U.S. Commission on Organization of the Executive Branch of the Government, *Research and Development in the Government*, A Report to the Congress, May, 1955.

rary world of hot and cold wars, to divorce science from political power in this country is to abdicate to totalitarian governments this basic power system of nature; and this, in turn,
would be to deprive ourselves of the very weapons we must have
to be strong enough to bring about negotiation for peaceful coexistence, or, should negotiation fail, to assure survival in the
event of war.

Or take the situation when the power of science is joined
with the power of industry. From this union flows everything
from cars to coat hangers, a continuous beneficence for material abundance, health, and cultivated living. Yet the
juncture of these two powers, resulting in the civilization of
which we are a part, proliferates still other moral problems:
the danger of overemphasis on materialism and practical results, the danger of industrial dislocation and of dying communities, the danger of a variety of human maladjustments,
unemployment, neurotic tensions, the ubiquitous effort to keep
up with the Joneses.

Everywhere, therefore, that we turn to pick up the thread
of the problem enmeshing us we find the older powers of government and of business now interweaving with that of science,
the most amoral of those powers, to compound and intensify the
dilemma with which our generation is bedeviled.

Nor can we miss the significance contained in the fact that
it has been the discovery—and the harnessing—of atomic energy
which has come, above any other single event of our time, to
symbolize the new place of science in the whole flow of American life. For, certainly, in the outpouring of almost bewitched
and awesome discussion through which our generation has been
contemplating the atomic and hydrogen bombs—not to mention
supersonic jets, guided missiles, and earth satellites—no one
can be left in doubt that here we stand finally face to face

with power at its most overwhelming destructiveness. Nor can
we escape issues of the gravest moral responsibility implicit in
the possession of such power. Yet merely to know the dimensions of the crisis precipitated by the bombs is not enough to
tell us how most effectively to deal with them. For the bombs
mark but a single point in a convoluted process, and it is the
process itself—the transformation of power from one form to
another—rather than any single point, that calls for a morality
and a power that checks destructive, in favor of productive,
uses.

Atomic energy latest link in chain of discovery

Atomic energy, then, though a revolutionary event, represents in a crucial sense only the latest link in a chain of discovery tracing back to the steam engine, and perhaps even before that to primitive man learning how to make fire with a
flint and stick. Its focal ties with science, moreover, are double-
stranded, reaching back (1) through the concepts and the
equations of nuclear physics to the whole cumulative stock of
scientific knowledge and (2) through the engineering skills
and practical know-how of the tinkering craftsman to the chain
of applied invention that has yielded the multiple tools and
goods of modern industry.[1]

While nuclear fission, therefore, undoubtedly dramatized
the new directions in the moral crisis of power, it cannot be
denied that the changes made so dramatically vivid by that
event were taking form long before World War II, and still

[1] Cf. Conant, James Bryant, *Modern Science and Modern Man*, pp.
23–35, Columbia University Press, New York, 1952. Thus, the Ein-
steinian formula $E = mc^2$, and the theories regarding interconvertibility
of matter and energy, could not be deemed really proved until the uranium
pile had yielded its practical large-scale manufacturing demonstration.

retain a pervasive influence in the organization of science and technology. We must accordingly chart out the shape of things to come in terms of these portentous developments of the past decades.

Moral implications in scientific research as a continuing, organized activity

Remembering that the activities of science and technology make available a distinctive and essential category of power, the discovery of the atomic bomb made it clear that a new development had taken place in the modern scientific quest. This outgrowth was the new role of research, which had become now an organized mobilization of skills and resources for the planned pursuit of a defined goal. In contrast to the episodic innovations turned up by lone inventors during the nineteenth century, organized research had here become a Leviathan, utilizing college laboratories, huge specialized plants, and thousands of skilled craftsmen. The question then becomes: Will such research constitute the dominant pattern of scientific technology in America in the years ahead? If, as seems probable, the answer is yes, what does this development portend for our moral crisis of power?

The new organization of research, moreover, not only enlisted individuals of diverse skills and training in science but also required separate, distinctive contributions from the other two systems as well. Not only scientists and technologists had to be recruited, but also management personnel from major business corporations, with their staffs and employees, along with the unions which represented the latter in bargaining. Finally, at the helm stood the state through the Federal government, alone able to supply the resources adequate to finance such costly projects, and thus possessing the power to define objectives, civilian as well as military, to formulate directives, and to mobilize and uproot men and transplant them into new and untried work environments. The division of function which operates in American industry was thus made unmistakably clear in a wartime project. What does it hold for the continuing issues of our troubled day?

Science raises again issue of individualism versus collectivism

In spite of this trend toward organization in scientific research, science has remained one of the few last arenas of individualism. It is one of the few places in which genius flourishes best when left to itself; the creative scientist–like the creative artist–cannot find fulfillment in an atmosphere of regimentation. With both industry and government drawing upon the faculties and staffs of universities and foundations, as well as recruiting available scientific personnel into their own research staffs, grave issues have been created for the individuals involved–issues usually inherent in the old dichotomy, organization versus individualism. In the face of present restrictions, one is not surprised to find Einstein saying shortly before he died that if he had his life to live over again, he would rather be a plumber than a scientist. For in his work community the scientist seeks, above all, freedom to carry on his work, to submit the results for independent verification by competent colleagues wherever they may be, and thus to exchange findings both within and across national boundaries. This freedom is essential if the fulfillment of talent, drive, and creativeness is to be achieved.

But what freedom can be preserved if one has to fit in with

plans, goals, and a policy of secrecy predetermined by external authority? The need for secrecy is particularly disturbing, yet it is inevitably implied in the race to develop military weapons. In industry the need of secrecy is more limited, it is true, because of the existence of patent rights. And the sheer logic of business—realizing profits on investments—impels emphasis on new products such as television, synthetic fabrics, new drugs, as well as utilizing new methods and machines for greater productivity. Nevertheless, the objectives of research, the amounts appropriated, the size of staff, and the like are defined by the corporation, that is to say, by business management. While the voice of the director of research is important in these decisions, in a final analysis it cannot be decisive. The crucial decisions are inevitably made on economic grounds.

Ethical implications of government subsidization and control as contrasted with business

At first glance, accordingly, it may look as if scientists face pressures to direct their work in ways determined by those who exercise political or economic power. Thus they become subject to compulsions directed toward "product" research. The pressures exerted by business, however, seem now to induce less ethical recoil than those emanating from government. The scientist still may feel concern about business' preoccupation with "product research," but the more forward-looking corporations have recently made it a practice to afford scientists their lead. Wallace Carruthers, for instance, investigating at Du Pont the structure of substances of high molecular weight, unlocked the discovery from which synthetic textiles have since flowed. At the very least, business promotes the uses of the new products developed by research, which in the long run assures the mass abundance rated high among the values of industrial society. Similarly, in government projects, while our attention has in recent years been riveted on military weapons, we should not forget the beneficence yielded by science in those agencies promoting better materials, better food, better public health. The attack on malaria and pellagra, on typhoid and smallpox, are only dramatic examples of the great contributions made by teams of scientists engaged in devoted service for the public good. It is the emphasis on national security in a divided world rather than government itself which has radically altered the whole tradition of scientific method and resulted in new products of such concentrated potential for evil and destruction as man has rarely before imagined.

War gives demonic accent to power of science

If the auspices, therefore, under which science has so recently been transformed seem to bring it squarely before a sharpened moral challenge, in that government, rather than business, projects the evil potentials, the emergent dilemma is much more complex than any such clear-cut divergence would suggest. It is true that the bomb which furnished the goal of the planned organized research not only dramatized the technical revolution in the workaday activities of the scientist but also suggested that man may have turned Frankenstein to create a modern uncontrollable superman bent on total destruction. The atomic and the hydrogen bombs stand forth for our own generation as the distillate of the demonic potential in science, for in them we hold tools of our own making that might in the end destroy us and the world we live in.

Yet, just as there is nothing new for modern men in the

process of technological innovation—whatever changes its planned, organized, continuing pursuit may induce—so there is nothing really new in the revelation that the products of technical advance may be used for evil as well as good. The products themselves, and the science behind them, are amoral—ethically neutral. Any innovation, as we have seen, may work good—or evil—among the men that make it and for whom they make it. The automobile that provides greater comfort in life may also become, as an armored vehicle or tank, an instrument of death. Similarly, the atomic bomb had been sought to bring victory in war against ruthless foes. Might it not be that war itself—however unavoidable in defense of freedom—rather than the bomb is what constitutes the quintessence of evil? From this viewpoint, the bomb again represents the most recent link in a chain of American inventions for war needs, as for peace, that absorb their freightage of good and evil from the uses to which they are put. Thus so characteristic and fertile an American procedure as mass production can be traced to Eli Whitney's program for manufacturing the flintlock muskets required by the young democracy in the threatening shadows of war with Napoleon's France. Similarly, we already know in our own twentieth-century era that nuclear energy may be turned also to the beneficent uses of peacetime. The swords we beat into plowshares and the spears into pruning hooks may be the tanks turned into tractors, the bombs into machine energy: but the conversion still waits on the day nation shall not lift up sword against nation, neither shall they learn war any more.

Moral issue involved in use of products of science

Beyond even this future ideal, the moral issues transcend the bombs themselves. We recoil, true, as we ponder their ethical

implications, but may it not have been better for the world that
we beat the Nazis in the race for that weapon? Again, how
much has the potential power it represents acted as a deterrent
to possible aggression on the part of the men in the Kremlin?
Nor should we forget that the bomb has also yielded the *technical* knowledge of how to harness the same energies for the
beneficent uses of medicine and industrial production. Iso-
topes are already an asset in medical clinics as well as in industrial technology. For the time being, in comparison with coal,
oil, and water power, only relative costs stand in the way of
atomic heat and energy. Clearly, after science chalks up its own
distinctive technical gains, the real moral challenge arises not
so much from past decisions as from those of the future, a multi-
tude of decisions still to be formulated concerning the best
use of the powers now made available.

The concrete issues boil down, then, to questions of *who*
shall decide, and *how, why, when*. Who shall make the decisions necessary to determine the directions of scientific research and particularly the use of results when vast expendi-
tures and many trained men must be enlisted in its programs?
How shall such decisions be arrived at and by what tests and criteria shall alternative courses and timing of action be evaluated? And, finally, by what powers shall such decisions be
enforced?

The same moral issues emerge from research promoted
primarily by business enterprise. It is easy to uncover the contrasts in objectives that wrap such a government project as
the bomb with a secrecy alien to scientific activity, while even
the familiar restrictions of patent rights do not overcome the
competitive drive to assimilate and market the flow of innovations—synthetics, TV sets, motor cars, air conditioning, and all
that goes to make up our rising standard of living and com-

fort. Yet, if costs emerge as criteria in projects that yield the bombs–so costly that only the Federal government could supply adequate financing–costs are similarly prime factors in industry. The sole exception occurs when several competitors are eager to make the market first, as in the race for a feasible transmitter of color television. However developed, the products of business research remain as ethically neutral as those of government until they are put to use. Then, and only then, does the content of their programs generate the serious issues of employment, of security, of aesthetics, of child rearing, of impact on cultural development. It is, however, when government or industry utilize these new products that a greater danger emerges. For here, in their utilization for war, hot and cold, for propaganda, and for politics, lies the possibility of the manipulation of men's minds. Thus do contemporary dictators add to the spirit of old-style tyranny the improved techniques of new-style instruments of communication, which may in a fundamental way prove even more demonic than the nuclear arsenal. For man's mind is still his most precious possession and, for the world, its greatest prize. Once more, therefore, the moral implications in the dilemmas created by modern research emerge in issues regarding the uses of its technically successful projects. And, once more, it is not science as such that is the greatest danger, but the coincidence of the coercions of government, exploiting evil potentialities in a science that is itself ethically neutral.

Yet, even this hypothesis–vexatious enough in all truth–cannot be accepted as full measure of the moral crisis of the twentieth century. For, if the decisions concerning the uses of power flowing from science seem increasingly, under the tensions of cold and hot war, to implicate government with the evil and business with the beneficent potentialities of technology, such divergence represents in reality a symbolic explanation of all our breaks with an earlier era of industrial expansion.

The first half of this century, the years that witnessed both the rapid development of organized research, the impact of total war, and the rise of the totalitarian states, also witnessed reforms to meet the social problems revealed by the great depression—reforms seen as a moral responsibility of society generally. It was recognized that a technically progressive society would inevitably bring various and recurring crises in family and community life. The fact that the assumption of social responsibility in the depression thirties came simultaneously with an explosion of conflicts between unions and corporations at home, and among nations abroad, inevitably meant that many dilemmas of power appeared. New moral problems involving augmented powers in the hands of labor, farmers, and government agencies were created even as the newer attitude of responsibility resolved older ones.

Nor do we gauge the full interpenetration during that period of social responsibility with technological change if we focus only upon the most widely discussed and familiar measures to meet unemployment, fluctuations in wage income, displacement, regional shifts of production, ghost towns, superannuation, sickness, and other social problems. For government undertook during those years a parallel underwriting of risks facing farmers, small businessmen, and, for a while, even financial institutions. What emerged as a fundamentally significant feature of this reorientation has been precisely the fact that the same political state which now mobilizes and finances organized research for the bombs is also the very instrumentality which cushions the injurious impact of industrial operation upon its citizens.

Thus the tendency is toward "bigness" in government, science, and business. But technical bigness in itself creates moral dilemmas. The very large-scale use of power calls for profound reorientations. Yet, whatever the power—be it that of science, government, business, labor, or agriculture—it remains essential to our society and it remains a source for potential good or evil, according to the uses to which it is put.

Predictability and visibility of impact of science

And with this we come to the final encompassing moral issue projected for us by the sheer transformation of science and technology from an individualistic, to a planned, organized, continuing activity interwoven with business and government. This is the existence of two tendencies which render inescapable the necessity to face up to the moral implications of the uses to which science is put. The first tendency may be termed that of *predictability*. While no one can safely claim that the progress of science is inevitable or assert with authority that as of such a time such and such an innovation will become available, it is yet true that in applied, as contrasted with pure, science, the probable direction of discovery emerging in any present stage of research can be charted with a fair degree of assurance. Thus, with the advent of radio, video was on the technical horizon; as black and white television spread, the race for color was already on. Again, no one can say with clearcut precision just when cost problems will have been sufficiently met to make nuclear energy a practicable source of industrial power, but the fact is inescapable that such a time does lie ahead. So, too, the assembly line leads to automation; and electronics makes possible automatic computation, communication, and controls of complex and ordinarily time-consuming projects.

The same shape of technological things to come is bound

up with equally foreseeable social problems–those arising in familiar dislocations and displacements, those arising out of the widening matrix of issues involved in the decisions about the use of the products of research–from the apocalyptic potentialities of the H-bomb to transistors, electronics, and so on. All past experience prepares us, for instance, for the backwash of "ghost towns," stagnant pools of regional decline, displaced craftsmen, hard-hit segments of industry (like electric trolleys, or coal mining, or textiles), as well as a host of aesthetic and emotional problems. Must not then our forecastable progress of organized research carry with it parallel preparation for meeting new and growing social responsibilities? And, if so, by whom shall these fundamental decisions be made? By what procedures shall they be projected? By what tests shall their adequacy then be evaluated?

The second tendency arising from the scientific revolution is that of *visibility*. Because of the very large-scale nature of scientific organization, other nations can see what we are doing and, more important, we can see ourselves as we truly are. Thus, if confidence in our democracy is to be maintained both here and abroad, we must have adequate procedures for meeting the consequences of our size. We are thus caught in a double but interrelated dilemma. On the one hand, we dare not in this power age call a moratorium on science if we wish to survive and preserve our standard of living. On the other hand, we cannot survive at all as a free society unless we address ourselves to the moral problems created by the industrial community of which science is a part. For without moral and ethical implementation in daily living we will inevitably lose faith in the worthwhileness of our own material achievement, no matter how prodigious, splendid, or chromium it may be.

5. *The power of business*

While science and technology give us mastery over the power yielded by nature, it is a mastery embodying only potential power to satisfy consumers' wants until business provides methods, tools, pilot plants, materials, motor power, appropriate marketing channels, and, of course, adequate capital to finance this complex of activities from beginning to end.

Business transforms scientific discovery into consumable goods

It would hardly appear any more necessary to review again the organic place of business in the sequence of functions making up the American economy with its outstanding productivity than to recall the role of science and technology as its wellsprings. It is everywhere apparent in the American scene that business and science are inextricably intertwined. Yet, from the viewpoint of our present-day moral crisis, it is precisely the blurring of this relationship that engenders some of our most grave and persisting perplexities. Ever since the assimilation of scientific advances into industry, for example, the gains due to science have been frequently ascribed to business management. When, by the same token, these gains can be realized only at the expense of hurtful dislocations, business has again been held responsible. It is thus business rather than science which has become the major target for blame by movements seeking to ameliorate the human cost of technical progress.

Contrasting positions of scientist and businessman

It is revealing to note the sharply contrasting positions into which these developments have brought the scientist and the business executive. From the dawn days of industrialism into our own immediate time, the scientist has seldom faced conflict over the value of his contributions to society. Secure in the approbation surrounding the advance of useful knowledge, the scientist and inventor have generally carried on their work in the relatively independent world of exploration into things as they are, building upon the ever growing stock of knowledge about the nature of things and adding to it by methods of inquiry approved by the scientific community. Sporadically, an inventor might show concern over the harmful potential of his discovery, as in the case of the brothers responsible for the mechanical cotton picker who hesitated to put it on the market because it would deprive so many hand pickers of the major source of their livelihood. Generally, however, the scientist could carry on his work without too much regard to the way in which the technical power he made available would be used.

With the discovery of the atom and hydrogen bombs, how-ever, moral concern has spread through the ranks of physical scientists and those associated with them in developing such lethal weapons. The work done in the study and laboratory still presents few qualms to the average scientist, though the changes wrought by the institutionalization of research, with the need for regimentation and secrecy, may alarm him. It is rather the use of the power they marshal, and not the power itself, that so profoundly disturbs so many of today's scientists —and all the rest of us.

The situation of business is markedly different. Since power and morality constitute, so to speak, the axis about which our dilemma centers, uncertainties regarding the position of busi-ness rise from both poles of this guide line. Scientists, in their perplexity over how to help bring about constructive, instead of destructive uses, may well attempt to dissociate themselves from the potential evil in their newest discoveries. Business-men, however, even if they so desired, cannot thus escape direct responsibility for social consequences.

With the increasing regulation by government and the massive expansion of trade unions beginning with the great depression, industry has been under constant fire to assume responsibility for the adverse human consequences of techni-cal progress, and to assimilate needed welfare measures into the cost structure of doing business. With some few exceptions, businessmen have generally resisted this pressure to assume these new, additional costs. Indeed, these measures for the most part have been imposed on corporate business by labor and government with the help of reformers and social workers. This resistance, however, need not be regarded as evidence of moral deficiency in businessmen, any more than the pres-sures for social gains are proof of exceptional virtue on the

part of union leaders and their members. We have been wit-
nessing rather the natural tugs of economic and political power
by groups acting in accordance with their interests and functions. The conflict and its results belong, as we shall see later,
to the characteristic American procedure of pressure, negotiation, compromise, and accommodation.

Contraction of business power

Businessmen urged to assume the increasing social responsibilities of technical progress must face, however, as we shall
presently see, an additional problem—the problem of whether
they should assume a greater burden than is technically practicable or even desirable. For precisely at the time when their
responsibilities have expanded, their prestige and influence—
that is to say, power—have paradoxically undergone a pro-
nounced contraction.

It furnishes one more index to the perplexities of our day
that such a statement, suggesting contracted business power,
will no doubt evoke far less immediate assent than the correlated thesis of expanded social responsibilities. For is it not
true that the power of industry is greater than ever before? The
fact is, however, that business has been functioning in a socially and politically hostile environment—a hostility that has
increasingly sharpened during the span of the current generation. On the face of it, ethical responsiblity connotes, in the
contemporary meaning of the term, an indefinitely expansible
program of social action, all of it a cost to business, while
power marks the very means for influencing attitude and behavior toward goals deemed desirable. It is surely evident that
business contributes to well-being not only by the goods and
services it makes available but also by the very measurable

requirements of wage increases, insurance premiums, fringe benefits, and so forth. But how is one to show that business power in American society has been contracted? Precisely what do we mean, indeed, by this business power?

It is patent, for instance, that business nowadays does not enjoy anything like the confidence granted science as a source of power essential to the modern community, and this in spite of the fact that corporate business is second only to government as a primary support of scientific research. Since invention and scientific discovery is at the very heart of the dynamic growth of American industry, business management must surely be regarded as a prime energizer in the advance of technological mastery.

Definition of technical power of business

What is the *technical power*, then, that business marshals for American society parallel to the technical power over nature made available by science and technology? To put it in a word, business harnesses economic power to the power of nature extracted as energy by science, so as to create goods and services for the community. The power of nature, released by science, is translated by business into energy-producing machines, tools, and services built and operated by men of varied skills in structured daily tasks—machines, tools, and services which carry forward the chain of activities that operate the many-layered entity we describe as *modern industry*.

Modern industry—an indirect, roundabout system of producing, distributing, and exchanging the goods and services by which we earn, enjoy, and expand livelihood—requires, throughout its linked extent, supervisors at the posts where the flow of work is directed and canalized to integrate the component factors of the process—capital, raw materials, steam and electric power, transport, and labor. All these must be successively assembled, integrated, and directed. With labor specialized, another task of integration must be accomplished—that of hiring, training, supervising. Variations of this generic managerial job appear in extractive enterprises such as farming and mining and in manufacturing, transportation, wholesaling, retailing, banking, utilities, education, social services, and so on through the multiple specialization characteristic of our society. The technical task of business management thus emerges as a characteristic job in administration in effectively handling multiple components of a continuing flow of activities directed toward defined ends. The technical power of economic administration marshaled by businessmen stands forth as a central instrument in the whole process of producing and distributing wealth, second only to the power of nature made available by science.

Defensiveness of business

Why, then, does the businessman seem to feel less confident than the scientist—so that his very aggressiveness in trying to justify his function seems in reality a symptom of defensiveness? Is it a phase of the declining influence and prestige already alluded to? Is the technical job of business more difficult to justify than that of science? There is a paradox in the fact that the answer to both questions must be in the affirmative. By all outward appearances the present-day structure of corporate business certainly suggests the same outstripping of early private enterprise as is found in present-day organized research in comparison with the lone inventors of the American past. To be sure, private business still dominates the field in the United

States, but it encompasses not only the individual, self-employed businessmen, small enterprises, and family establishments, but also large corporations in mining, manufacturing, marketing, insurance, and finance so huge as to constitute to all intents and purposes quasi-public organizations. This complexity, however, does not include all the factors we must reckon with in understanding the intrinsic character of the moral crisis we confront. For business, like science, spreads beyond its own functional boundaries—and much more pervasively. It reaches back into the function of research as we have already seen. More importantly, it reaches forward into the political system and becomes inextricably interwoven in diverse ways with political activities.

The business corporation, like all other collective forms in our society, itself functions politically. As such it encounters competing organizations—trade unions, for example—which impose restrictions upon management in making essential decisions. Again, growing legislative regulations and administrative procedures have progressively narrowed its range of policy making and execution. Peace and wartime demands by government for goods and services have established not only competitive price bidding but also standards for acceptable quality. The rise of the so-called public corporation, from the municipal utility to great multipurpose organizations like the Tennessee Valley Authority, has introduced a form of outright competition against business both in cost and comparative efficiency.

Finally, rival economic systems are now actually operating in other nations. Thus, competition has moved from the long academic debate between actual capitalism and theoretic socialism—to the everyday concrete operation of systems ranging from the state trusts of Soviet Russia to the nationalized in-

dustries of Western democracies, to the private business enterprise of this country. Thus, developments both here and abroad
during the past half century have tended to undermine the
influence and prestige of private business.

Difficulty in separating technical power from moral values

The prevailing climate of hostility adversely affects in yet
another way the position of private industry. In a technical
sense, economic administration, like science and technology,
emerges as one more natural function—as a system of power,
which integrates into productive units the component factors
necessary to satisfy man's wants. It is a system of power furthermore, which like the power of science is amoral, ethically
neutral. It would seem proper, therefore, that the businessman
might first concern himself with establishing operational efficiency and then consider the social consequences stemming
from his acts.

It would be well if the businessman, like the scientist and
technologist, could lay claim to any such bifurcated standards
for evaluating performance. It would enable all of us as
Americans to understand functions and responsibilities more
objectively. Thus, even though business continued to be criticized, it would be freed from the generalized hostility which
now prevails. It is all but impossible, however, for the business
executive to achieve the separation between technical and ethical responsibilities which is available to the scientist who sticks
to his last and lets others decide the appropriate use of his
discoveries. For business behavior *is* intrinsically less technical
than science; and, whereas the scientist always stops short of

human application, the businessman constantly confronts such application in every decision he makes. His everyday tasks carry him through the whole gamut of activities from the completely amoral to the completely moral. Thus, the technical "must" and the ethical "ought" are constantly intermingled. It indeed is important for all of us to understand the confusions with which this blurring surrounds business performance, precisely because these confusions implicate all Americans as we meet the world-wide trend to compare rival economic philosophies to the disparagement of the American system.

Business exercises power through men

The distinctive qualities of business activities that subject management, as contrasted with the scientist, at once to less measurable tests of effective work and to more immediate pressures of ethical responsibility, arise in the very nature of the technical power businessmen help marshal for their society. Let us recall that science makes available expanding powers over nature. Now the pursuit of knowledge concerning things as they are—the physical universe, its flora, fauna, stones, stars, energies, even man himself and his society—need never—indeed, by the norms of scientific method, should never—be deflected by consideration of things as they ought to be. Until the research workday is finished, the technical "musts" of "good" science do not collide with the ethical "oughts" of social responsibility; or, to put it differently, the values determining the drive of the scientist—the passion for truth, and mastery over brute fact—are also controlling norms in his job performance, and entirely compatible with the materials of his work. To be sure, the businessman also handles brute facts—raw materials, equipment, mechanical power, workplaces, transportation, markets—quite comparable to the engineer's preoccupation with material reality. But these impersonal elements are only part of his job: man constitutes an even more important factor. In terms of technical considerations, man's labor must be viewed impersonally, as an item of cost, an objective matter-of-fact element in the task of turning out wealth for the community. But the human being, as an acting part of any job content and as the ultimate recipient of the products of enterprise, inevitably introduces ethical criteria. He is never simply energy, skill, or purchasing power—but *man*, thinking, feeling, desiring, and aspiring. And, since all the technical facts filter into the business process through and toward men, it is hardly surprising that moral issues are seldom divorced from technical performance.

Moral values constantly challenge technical performance of business

The businessman must thus reckon with the consumer, the price- and quality-conscious beneficiary for whom the whole productive process is carried forward. So, too, he now must include considerations of employees who may be dislodged or otherwise adversely affected by innovations. These responsibilities furnish the familiar challenge of basically ethical values upon the technical tests for efficient performance. The question for business is: Are technically justifiable decisions made by management also ethically just decisions? Thus, economic administration in the United States, as elsewhere, is implicated with the whole social process. It is not enough to ask which system produces the most effective technical results; we must also ask what ethical values are promoted or sacrificed by the evolving changes everywhere transforming established economic ways. These questions are put by the men and their supervisors at the workbench, as well as by the political associations that variously represent them to the surrounding society in which and for which they do their jobs. All this results in contraction of managerial authority. At the opposite end of the range, in communist or fascist countries, the subordination of economic adminstration, as of all major activities, to the authority of political dictatorship results in compulsory obedience to "technical" decisions down the work line, no matter how unjust or onerous.

Profits as technical tests of business performance

The main test of technical proficiency in American democracy resides in the profit the enterprise earns. Profit manifestly constitutes a measurable criterion, one that can be seen and evaluated by the stockholders, and the business that fails to show a profit sooner or later fails to survive. Nonetheless, just as the rigor of this criterion is sharpened by the linkage of business with science and technology, so is it blunted by those forces that link managerial decisions with politics and ethics. For profit represents a residue–a figure arrived at after all the costs of operation are balanced against the income earned for service rendered at a given price per unit. But costs and profits in themselves are much more than that. They represent a symbol of complex individual and social human behavior–the choices and motivations of many human actors in our varied economic activities, such as market competition, supply, substitution, legal regulation, and the response to prices of the various satisfactions offered. Thus, we must evaluate the monetary figures always in terms of the men who supply material and equipment, the employees, union leaders, bankers, government officials, and, finally, the consumers, who allocate available funds among the ever growing variety of satisfactions offered for immediate use, or for savings and investments.

But, if costs and gains themselves summarize a variety of men who constantly act and make choices, they attain thereby a quality of imprecision that reflects the dynamic voluntarism of the unpredictable, intractable human agent. Neither costs nor prices, profits nor losses, are set, fixed measures; instead, they are contractible and expansible, with changing conditions and under varying pressures. It is an explicit objective of American management so to improve and raise productivity that ever more satisfactions will be available at relatively declining prices to masses of men possessing relatively increasing income for purchasing them. Indeed, ever increasing productivity is itself a long-run social test of technical performance; thus does American business justify our industrial system. But the continuing shorter-run effects of profits and costs raise grave questions on the adequacy of this test. If it remains part of the administrator's task in each enterprise always to keep costs low and profits high, the effort immediately involves him in technical decisions that in the very nature of things cannot be precise. For how low is low, if costs are measured, not by the monetary factor alone, but by tests of economic soundness, of social responsibility, of ethical-human values? Moreover, since costs summarize a wide miscellany of requirements, what items are contractible, and which fixed and over how long a time span? What expedients should be utilized for reducing costs: Layoffs? New suppliers? Improved equipment? Removal of plant to lower-cost regions? And by what tests should such decisions be made?

Any attempt to answer such questions immediately reveals

how business performance is less submissible than science to precise technical criteria. Yet, if judgment is to be exercised in choosing courses from among available alternatives, that judgment should be based on as firm a foundation of relevant knowledge as possible. Admittedly such knowledge can never be complete, nor can decisions wait upon the acquisition and testing of all the facts.

Lack of verifiable tests in business as compared to science

While the scientist also accepts all new knowledge as tentative and characteristically presents his results within boundaries of "standard error," those results are at some time verifiable not only through acceptable control methods but also independently by other students in the field. Managerial judgment and decision, on the other hand, together with the facts upon which decisions are based, cannot be submitted to comparable tests. Granting the availability of testing devices, private enterprise is so dynamic that the policy implemented to meet a given business problem—declining markets, expanding ones, new products, competitive products, seasonal demand—cannot, by and large, be suspended while alternative courses are tested as a control on results. Nor can the components of a business situation be so isolated and duplicated that executives of other companies can, in a scientific sense, verify the policy from their own experience. A chosen course, moreover, may even achieve the technical objective of continuing the stability of the enterprise and of earning a sound profit without at any time attaining the sanction extended to the scientist when a technical performance is rated acceptable by the standards of science. The consequences of managerial decisions, finally, however firmly grounded and technically sound, encounter challenges quite different from any that yet confront the scientist. These challenges, political and moral in their nature, not only render it difficult to do what may be technically necessary but also limit the authority of management in making any decision.

Self-interest versus community interest

The centrality of financial return has exposed the business system as an easy target both to traditional moral questioning and the newer winds of radical doctrine that have been loosening so many of our attitudes from their wonted moorings. For one thing, the return available to owners of an enterprise still constitutes the ultimate test in deciding whether it is or is not well managed. Again, however much one may concede the high productivity of American industry, however much we may point to the wide distribution of corporate ownership, the fact also remains that business executives enjoy the highest incomes of any group in the nation. And from earliest times rich men have been customary objects of envy and hostility.

Finally, rare indeed is the businessman who does not find himself frequently in situations of moral conflict. How and where is he to draw the line between social responsibility and self-interest? He may be certain that on the basis of the best available data the business outlook compels layoffs of workers, or reduction of inventories, or completely new machines requiring fewer employees, or concentration of production in particular low-cost mills. Thus ethical "oughts" become clouded in the face of the technical "musts" in any critical decision as to solvency and profitability. Furthermore, quite apart from the businessman's own position as manager, the fact that he holds office at the will of a board of directors and of the stockholders introduces an inevitable bias in favor of financial prudence when interpreting "the best available data." For it is not, as in the scientist's world, his technical peers but the owners and their representatives who, threatened with possible losses, render judgment upon the executive and his methods of operation—not indeed always in terms of objective facts and moral values but rather in terms of self-interest.

Thus it remains unreal and impractical to expect a corporation to operate with equal proficiency as a technical tool mobilizing economic and scientific power to produce goods and services *and* as a social institution with human beings depending upon it both inside and outside its gates. If power is a necessity to maintain and increase our standard of living, management's first responsibility must always be to maintain the enterprise in good economic health; that is to say, its power must be kept at the highest level of efficiency. Certainly, one must not risk bankruptcy. Thus, if, after careful and even painful consideration, transfer of a factory to a new location is the only way of survival, then move one must, regardless of the cost to the old community and its people. At best, only ameliorative measures may be applied, such as separation wages, help in finding other jobs, relief, and so on. Again, few if any enterprises have large enough resources to meet by themselves the impact of severe unemployment, or old age, or serious illness. To spend resources to meet total social needs might indeed imperil the corporation as a productive tool, so that it could no longer serve its main purpose of creating goods and services. To put it in terms of this book, the power a business enjoys to carry out its primary mandate would be dissipated. Thus, self-interest puts a premium on managerial competence and effectiveness, so that in the end, while some individuals and even certain communities may be adversely affected, the power exercised is more likely over the long run to bring the best results to the whole society by making possible increasing wealth and well-being.

Stated baldly, as it has been so far in this analysis, it sounds as if businessmen and their collaborators are insensitive to human needs. Of course, nothing of the kind is meant. We are simply trying to isolate their function as technicians administering a system of power, just as we would the function of engineers operating equipment that generates steam, or electric, or nuclear power. Indeed, businessmen today are already meeting an ever increasing load of human responsibility. But this assumption of added responsibilities and correlative costs is due primarily to forces generated by political and moral power.

Thus, in 1949, the steel corporations were reluctant to agree to a system of noncontributory old age pensions, as were the automobile companies to the so-called Guaranteed Employment Plan or the supplementary unemployment benefit plans in 1955. It was not that they were opposed *as citizens* to adequate measures against the hazard of old age and unemployment. The heart of their argument was that the problems of old age and unemployment should be met by government provision, through Social Security benefits and unemployment compensation, respectively, rather than by individual corporations. In the end, they yielded to plans which, in effect, supplemented government provisions; but they yielded only because of countervailing political and economic power exerted by the trade unions concerned—in 1949 by an actual strike, in 1955 by a potential strike. Thus, according to our analysis, their thinking was sound; it was not their function to assume huge social expenses over an extended period. Problems which affect whole populations had better be met by the government on the principle of insurance—in this case, premiums imposed by taxes on corporations and individuals—the very essence of which is to pool a given risk so that no one individual is in danger of having to meet undue costs.

There is no escaping the implications, therefore, of the amorality of power as power in the business or economic world any more than in the world of science. Nor does it mean that as a community we let social needs go unmet. In modern America, as in all democracies—certainly by the mid-twentieth century—we no longer are content to let the "poor" stay poor, and the very dimensions of the power that science, business, and government now muster enables us confidently to say for the first time in man's long history that we need *not* always have the poor with us.

And so we turn next to our exploration of government as a system of power essential for meeting the social needs projected upon the community by the very efficiency in the use of power by both science and business.

6. *The power of government*

The fact that it is government, rather than science and industry, which must bear the major burden of alleviating the distress that goes with technological progress–since government alone, with its power to tax, can support programs adequate to meet major human needs–confronts us with a problem of the greatest magnitude. For government, far from being one among three equal power systems, constitutes the greatest power center of all, with the widest sweep of authority to compel obedience. Both the power of science and that of business are decentralized and limited. Science, indeed, so long as it remains in the laboratory, has no coercive force at all: it is only when its findings are converted into products or services that it acquires whatever coercive potential it knows.

Business wields a greater degree of coercive power, for it can deprive the community of goods and services, or employees of the opportunity to work, as a way of enforcing its decisions as to prices, wages, or other considerations. These depriva-

tions, however, constitute the outermost limit of coercion that
may be imposed; and even these face limits, for, in practice,
they can seldom be imposed to the full degree. A single business enterprise seldom possesses today the degree of monopoly
on goods or jobs necessary to wield such power, or, if it does
have such a monoply, it faces counterchecks through unions,
consumer groups, government agencies, or all three, which
make it impossible or unwise to use its power to the full. The
risks are too great. Moreover, under normal circumstances,
employees and customers have a range of alternative choices.
They are free to refuse to work or to buy, just as the businessman may refuse to employ or sell.

Government alone possesses
complete coercive power

In sharp contrast, government alone enjoys supreme sovereign power. It alone may exercise the whole gamut of coercive powers, including the extremity of imprisonment and
death, provided of course that constitutional procedures, or
"due process," are observed. At the same time, because it falls
to the state to meet the human needs left by science and business, human values, with all their ethical and moral overtones,
are easily claimed as the goals of government. Thus, the coercive harshness of the state becomes softened with the glow of
benevolent promise. Indeed, politicians seeking to gain and
hold office naturally exploit these moral goals.

Politics, it should be remembered, embodies in the main the
power of men over men. Scientists make available power over
nature, in which man himself is only indirectly involved. Business mobilizes the energy of applied science through machines
and men. In the political function, however, man dominates the

whole activity, and is at once the source of the power, the direct instrumentality through which it is wielded, and the presumed beneficiary for whom it is exercised. Yet no other power now looms more menacing or more difficult to control. For the controls sought must, as we have seen, find an uneasy, ever shifting balance between unfilled needs on the one hand and the threat of absolutism on the other.

Indeed, it is the national state which is the chief source of our fear today—in the propensity of modern governments to carry men once more into the maw of absolutism. The fear inheres, not only in the already-mentioned fact that government alone possesses the powers to invoke physical sanctions to compel obedience, but also in the fact that the dictatorially-minded politicians who today seize the machinery of government seize with it the instruments of communication, education, economics, science, industry, law, army, police, and social services. They thus make themselves absolute. The tide of events in recent decades has caught mankind in an undertow, dragging the twentieth century from the moorings established by man's brief venture into freedom and democracy back to the ancient depths of tyranny. The case for alarm thus practically writes itself.

Interest groups and the drift toward centralism

Yet this apparent drift to statism does not contain the whole story. For, within democracies, during these same years interest groups—labor unions, corporations, farmers, and others—have both promoted and revealed a similar tendency. In their constant effort to invoke government support for their respective programs, they have pushed the state into ever wider regulation of economic and social life. Moreover, within some of these organizations, the same drift toward centralization of power has been seen, as for instance, in the expanded role of the union leader. Finally, the drift toward centralism within groups has been essential to their attempts to acquire an ever greater influence in the national economy as a whole. As a result, large extensions of government activity have occurred not only during the depression of the 1930s and the war of the 1940s but also well before those crisis years, at times when business corporations through their lobbies were acquiring augmentations of power quite comparable in their narrower sphere to the growth of state authority in its more comprehensive, sovereign reach. The problems projected by lobbies have received considerable attention. What we wish to emphasize here, however, is that these probings into interest organizations have carried overtones of ethical criticism, portraying these groups as threats to democracy in its function as guardian of the public interest.

Our experience during the tumultuous years since 1930, however, has compelled a revision of this initial interpretation. For one thing, it requires little demonstration that powerful labor unions, which have now spread their influence through the economy, are themselves essentially political organizations. Even before their recent swift growth, students of the structure of the labor movement were presenting trade unions as a species of politics both in their internal and in their external operations. The election of officers, the relationships between leaders and followers, the constitutions and bylaws, the political machines, the formulation and administration of union policies, all spell out the familiar political designs—with their characteristic variations.

But business organizations, quite as much as unions, also present their aspects of political activity. The watchful eye maintained by subordinates upon their superiors, the formation of alliances, coalitions, and cliques, the emergence of bureaucratic administration–the pervasive activities of employers' and trade associations as well as chambers of commerce in local, state, and national levels–such features of modern business enterprise are now familiar and accepted. Nor is it difficult to trace the same characteristics of political behavior in associations representing farmers, veterans, and the professions.

The power aspects of interest groups

The uniformity in all such associations lies in the marshaling of the political power of groups to safeguard and advance common objectives, a uniformity of group power with a wide range of variation. Individual labor unions, for instance, range from such centralized power structures as the United Mine Workers to organizations such as the International Typographical Union with its established provision for party opposition. Business corporations, while naturally reflecting the technical requirements of shop discipline and executive authority in decision making, nevertheless range (as this is written) from the highly centralized type of administration prevailing in Montgomery Ward to the decentralized one in General Motors. But, beyond all the variations in the specific organization of power, these group associations represent both important instruments of the whole political process and strategic sectors in the American system of political behavior.

The same experience, however, which arouses concern over the effects of these pressure blocs in compelling more extensive government activity, reveals also a modifying influence springing from the very strength of these groups. For, as each is watchful of the other, and all watchful of government, they checkmate one another and the state. The nub of the matter can be put in a summary contrast. By the mid-twentieth century, a combination of profound forces set our workaday industrial activities in a new context of social responsibilities, defined and enforced by government intervention in a series of reforms that wrote a long-gathering moral challenge into the ways of doing business. As we look back upon the 1930s and the 1940s, it is easier now than then to realize that business almost inevitably had to undergo the period of criticism and abuse which was to baffle and outrage a newer, professionally-minded management corps. In the atmosphere, first, of economic stagnation, and then, of defense and war, in which government measures held prime place, business was slow and reluctant to adjust to its new role.

But, if its power was thereby contracted, events soon made it clear that it had at the same time recaptured a position of considerable influence. If unionism and collective bargaining were affirmed as public policy, business nevertheless proved strong enough to resist excessive demands at the negotiating table and to promote a campaign in individual states and in Washington for statutory and administrative curbs upon the expanding power of labor. The Wagner Act gave way to Taft-Hartley. In a considerable number of states "right-to-work" laws checked or replaced statutes modeled on the original Wagner Act.

By the 1950s, the scene had changed, with a Republican administration replacing the Roosevelt-Truman regime. A new balance of power accordingly was established. While business found itself again in a friendly atmosphere, labor was not thereby dislodged from its newly established status. It remained an equal partner, in the social structure of the nation.

But its aggressiveness had been curbed. It was to be an equal–
not a dominant–partner. With this shifting balance, government too changed its position. As the Eisenhower administration felt its way, it withdrew from active participation in the
varying tugs of power between industry and labor. Thus, in
contrast to the constant intervention of the White House in
strategic strikes during the Roosevelt and Truman administra-
tions, two major strikes–the Southern Telephone and the Louis-
ville and Nashville–were settled in 1955 without involving the
President's office.

It is such group associations which in the United States will
carry forward political activity in the closing half of our century. For the mobilization of group power to promote group
objectives is the distinctive character of political behavior.
Certainly the group that is the whole American society must be
differentiated from those special constituencies comprised of
wageworkers, businessmen, farmers, and all the rest. But precisely because, when the United States was launched as an independent nation, its founders consciously and deliberately
developed procedures for group interaction and decision making, we may recognize the basic political processes that char-
acterize both the special-interest association and the formal
government agency.

The tests of adequate performance
applied by rank and file

The basic procedures of political activity, and the framework about which organized political power is mobilized, belong to the subject matter of evolving political theory. We shall
here touch only upon those aspects that illuminate the contemporary moral crisis. In so far as political organization mar-

shals the power of associated men for promoting a common objective, it also revolves about relationships between the ranks
who constitute its membership and their leaders. In our large-
scale society, the actual formulation of policy is delegated to
the leadership; the rank and file presumably pass upon the
satisfactory quality of the results achieved in terms of the interests to be served. Thus, Congress makes the laws, and the
people show their satisfaction or lack of it by the way they vote
in subsequent elections.

The actual making of the rules for any group activity produces its particular brand of legislative representatives, such as
delegates to conventions, boards of directors, executive councils, faculty committees, elected congressmen or state legislators. Continuing administrative needs result in an organizational bureaucracy. Disagreements on rights, equities, and
obligations are resolved by judicial procedures. Specialized
agents are appointed to enforce the rules. Party, police, military, beaucracy—these power instruments—become themselves
problems of power in times of trouble and transition. But, beyond all the complexities due to specialization in formulating,
promoting, and carrying forward programs, we come back always to the political axiom that the rank and file constitute the
ultimate judges upon the success of given leadership policies
launched in their name.

Difficulty of formulating tests
of political performance

In these circumstances, one might ask what tests, what criteria, may be applied to evaluate the technical proficiency of
political performance. Certainly not the rigid tests available to
scientists, nor the even more flexible but still quantitative tests

of costs and efficiency available to the business executive. In politics, it would seem no such tests apply. The thought, however, is an arresting one, especially when we recall that the very connotations of "technical tests" imply judgments by measures specifically related to, or appropriate to, the activities involved. For, manifestly, politics, quite as much as science and business, possesses its technical skills.

Politicians and labor leaders alike we rate as being more or as being less "effective," "responsible," and so on. The whole country, for instance, witnessed an example of the need for political "know-how" when it watched President Eisenhower and his team of businessmen fumbling about as they sought to acquire the essentials of their new jobs during the first years of office. President Roosevelt, again, was known as a "consummate" politician, not in an invidious sense but rather in that of being a political leader who knew how to get his programs through Congress. Thus, the "strong" executive has become a model, so to speak, in the annals of American history.

The very lack of further tests for evaluating political performance, however, may well stem from the basic character of politics itself. For one thing, political activity is concerned preeminently with problems of wealth distribution. Just as scientific technology and business are concerned primarily with the production of wealth, so politics is primarily concerned with the health and safety underlying the conditions of production and with the equitable distribution of the national product among all valid claimants. These issues—problems of how much, when, why, and for what ends, the products of industry should be allocated—manifestly raise technical as well as ethical questions. But, unlike the situation in science and industrial management, which enjoy tangible measures as a base for evaluating performance, standards of performance in politics

are implicated rather with the incommensurable, illimitable
desires of the electorate, the rank and file, whose claims the
office seeker aims to satisfy.

Moral ambiguities of politicians

Accordingly, the politician is constantly confronted with
moral ambiguities much more troublesome than those encoun-
tered by the business executive. For while the latter, in deciding upon alternative policies, faces the temptation of self-interest as against wider community needs, nevertheless he
cannot and must not play fast and loose with the economic facts
of the business situation. In contrast, the politician, in order to
gain and hold office, that is to say, power, is constantly tempted
to play down facts which may counsel an unpopular course of
action. Thus, while the businessman may be amoral in making
his decisions, the politician may, in glossing over the truth,
actually and frequently teeter onto the immoral side of behavior. He may make promises that he knows he will never be
able to fulfill, accusations that he knows to be unfounded, com-
parisons that he knows to have only the slighest foundation in
fact. Individual differences emerge, of course; but all politicians aspire to gain, hold, and advance in office. The aim thus
centered upon political power is directed by many varying convictions and ideals. And so we get the statesman as well as the
demagogue, the dictatorial union leader as well as the dedicated one, the inspiring corporation executive as well as the one
who rules by fear and terror. But, by whatever methods and
qualities the politician gained his office, he must—whether he
is president of a club or president of his country—serve the
specific group interests for which he speaks.

This requirement presents grave ambiguities, however, at

the level of government. Spokesmen for trade associations, labor unions, and farm and professional associations, with the development of regulatory legislation of lobbies, carry their prime mandate more and more by open identity. Representing men of common concerns, speaking in policy-making sessions with representatives of other groups, or speaking through established channels to the general public, these spokesmen are marked agents of defined special interests. Government officials, on the other hand—elected to enact and execute laws, and serving presumably as guardians of the public interests—must face the fact that each owes his office, first, to the citizens in his particular locality, who, secondly, comprise among their number spokesmen for diverse organized interests. As an individual, the politician can retain power only according to the quality of his performance on both levels of responsibility. Nor is the politician's task made any easier by the fact that organized minorities make their voices heard with a volume and at times a raucousness that drowns out the more amorphous and vague unorganized call to public interest.

The "musts" and the "oughts" of political behavior

It is in the political party that the interacting compulsions, the "musts" and the "oughts" of political behavior, find their true home. The preoccupations of politics with the power of office, like that of science with discovery and business with efficiency, constitute the life blood of political enterprise. A politician may now and then operate as a "maverick," an independent. But careers are predominantly promoted through party loyalty. To retain power, the officeholder must serve his party; he must also serve the regional and bloc interests which have elected him and which constantly scrutinize his record of daily performance. Even the party program must adjust to the divergent tugs of these interests as they seek to make their influence felt at the level of the party organization. Since the pinnacle of power toward which all politicians aim, however, is control of the majority administration at the national level, parties and officials alike must try—at least, in verbal profession—to make their continuing actions square with the larger public interest of which they are the guardians.

Manifestly, such conflicting standards for evaluating performance make it very difficult to submit concrete conduct in politics to tests of technical effectiveness and ethical standards. What is effective in serving local or regional interests may be ineffective to a party seeking unity; what may be effective for the party, may alienate support in the region and so on. Appeals for support and loyalties are in reality nothing but exchanges of promises. Candidates characteristically outbid one another in the respective benefits they undertake on behalf of organized groups, while pledging loyalty to the general good to which everyone subscribes in a general way but about which no one group is vigilant. Such promissory notes on the future, moreover, are accompanied by another particular currency of political exchange. Since the short-term view demands policies slanted to particular interests, skills arise for "explaining" away the unexpected and the unsatisfactory. Thus politicians typically claim credit for all that goes as the constituency would have it go, and place blame for failures on the opposition—be it the minority party, the other party in collective bargaining, the "government" and its "bureaucrats," the internal "faction" of organization, "Wall Street," the monopolists, or whatever symbol of hostility best serves to deflect the dissatisfactions in varying situations. At government levels, the two-party system furnishes the administration in office a visible op-

ponent, and the opposition a parallel target for free-wheeling
criticisms in its own strategy of power.

Temptation to manipulate emotions as a way of gaining power

Electioneering, propaganda, even manipulation–appeals
and arguments directed to emotions and passions rather than to
the objective merits of the case–these techniques produce at
best questionable results. Like all techniques, they contain an
amoral potential dependent upon the manner of their use. At
times they seem no more than humorous explosions in a continuous Fourth of July parade, yet a grave peril to democracy
inheres in the manipulation of emotions, of fears, of hopes, and
of aspirations to which political communication is often re-
duced. For these emotions are canalized through the finest
ideals of the community; the patriotism that long has been
recognized as "the last refuge of a scoundrel" becomes in
modern political dress the first recourse of the demagogue–or
the dictator. Thus it is that the mechanics of power in the political universe tend so strikingly to the immoral. Amoral as is
all power in its genesis, standards for right action remain so
amorphous in politics that manipulation of fact and feeling
finds a natural haven as it never can in science and technology,
and only with great difficulty in business. Time and again, the
methods of a demagogue bear a disturbing similarity to the
power techniques of the latter-day totalitarians; tocsins of
alarm may well be sounded.

Dangers in amorality of political power

Thus, again, the circle rounds itself. Political power, the
power of the group, much as all power, is in its genesis amoral,

ethically neutral. But even more than the power of nature uncovered by science, or the economic power of business organized into modern industry, the amorality of group power projects the most profound dangers when concentrated in the hands
of a few. For, while the state's leaders represent the power of
sovereign rights, of coercion and command, even of life and
death, their performance cannot easily be submitted to tests
either of technical proficiency or of justice. Political behavior,
instead, reckoning accomplishment in the coin of promises,
verges frequently on the immoral. It is not difficult, as a result,
to issue warnings in terms of the portentous parallels between
the demagogue and the dictator, between the "bigness" of our
own state and the monolithic finales of the totalitarian state.

Yet, government, as we have seen, has financial, as well as
moral, responsibility for meeting human needs beyond resources of private enterprise. Political power, we know from
historical experience, holds the potential for positive good, as
well as for absolute evil. Moreover, it is difficult to envisage in
our complex society a condition under which science and business may eliminate the backwash of social problems left in the
wake of their very progress. There will always be gaps in human needs for government to provide. Thus, a wise citizenry
must urge upon the state the assumption of human tasks and at
the same time the utmost vigilance to safeguard the sanctioned
and "built-in" curbs which rein and harness the forward push
of those who govern.

It is not by accident that historically the evil potential of
power has been associated primarily with the state. Thus, it
was to the Prince—not to business or science—that Machiavelli
addressed his advice on how to seize and hold power. So did
Lenin to the élite of the Communist Party. So did Hitler to the
storm troopers, and Mussolini to the Blackshirts. These three

latter-day tyrants also improved on Machiavelli by seizing industry, communications, and all the other apparatus essential for carrying on the modern life of the community. For the very logic of power in the state is the necessity of the powerful to remain powerful.

It was to the corollary inherent dangers that the founders of the nation addressed themselves in Philadelphia in 1791, and in the Federalist papers during the period of ratification. It is to these historic events that we shall presently refer for the lessons they teach on the stabilization and taming of power.

7. *The power of morality*

However complex may be the powers of science, business, or politics—amoral in their origins and capable of the greatest evil according to their uses—man as the administrator of these powers confronts in himself a power system more complex than any of these—the power of morality.

Man, however, is *born* amoral. His prime instinct is to live, to survive, perhaps to dominate. At the very moment of birth, he exercises his power to cry with anger and rage—the only power at his command. The human being is made up of a physiological mechanism that is alerted instantly by the emotions of fear and anger to the dangers of his environment and is highly adapted to the fight for survival. His autonomic, or sympathetic, nervous system works automatically, not only to take care of such normal functions as breathing, digesting, and ridding the body of waste, but also in the presence of danger to regulate a secretion of chemical substances (hormones) which heighten nervous stimuli and give him an even greater keenness in mobilizing his energies to fight. The body becomes slippery with sweat; the muscles are tensed for fight or flight. Moreover, these stimuli are relayed so rapidly to the muscles that a fighting stance is, to all practical purposes, instantaneous, preceding indeed even the mind's own swift awareness of danger.

Because he is thus born to exercise power, the power systems we have so far discussed—scientific, economic, and political— find a natural habitat in man. It is man who attempts to master nature by learning her secrets and applying them. And, since he has been equipped by nature to fight for self-preservation, man exercises his power primarily for his own interest. Primitive, primordial man had no alternative but to kill or be killed, to enslave or be enslaved, to rule or be ruled. But, as social organization began to develop, with the family, the clan, the tribe, all claiming their right to survive, man's powers of preservation and of reasoning could no longer be utilized solely in terms of self-interest. Economic and political power began to develop; for a world ordered for one man might not suit another; ordered for both, it might make each twice as strong. Group survival thus became the major consideration in the primitive world, even in the interest of individual self-preservation. And so we find even in primitive societies the development of rules, customs, rituals, in order that economic and political power may be socialized and limitations placed on its exploitation for selfish ends. In our own contemporary societies, man from the formative period of childhood on undergoes a continuous process of initiation, education, and conditioning to make him conform to the codes of the group.

Man, however, even with the autonomic nervous system given him by nature for survival is a physical weakling in the animal kingdom. But, fortunately, nature also equipped him with a brain, with unique centers for reflective conscious reasoning, by means of which he may master his instinctual life and direct his personal powers even beyond survival to larger and more complex goals transcending his immediate self-interest. Thus, he invents tools—that is, applies power—for enriching the material life of his group. He develops also logical and moral drives for preserving and enhancing the social life of his community. In fact, in our contemporary American society, man as the administrator of economic and political powers finds that he is the bearer of a highly sensitized moral self, saturated from childhood with the ethical, social, and religious codes of his society.

Conscience as agent of moral power

How does this power in human affairs express itself—this power which parallels that of nature marshaled by science, that of industry marshaled by business, or that of the group marshaled by politics? It is the power of conscience. And conscience is nothing other than the internalized system of beliefs, ideas, and sentiments which propels man toward moral goals in his conduct with his fellow man and his society. Conscience is the carrier and implementer of the gospel, both personal and social. Conscience is what keeps reminding man of his duty to God and his fellow man, what arouses in him fear of sin and love of virtue. Conscience is pervasive, never ceasing. It haunts man day and night in every social act he undertakes, or even considers undertaking. Nor can he escape it, even though he may believe he has fully rejected it.

How rigorously conscience presses its commands and imperatives has in recent years been borne in upon us by many diverse currents of thought. The revolt against the so-called

Puritan conscience has colored the attitude of, and the literature about, the generation between the two world wars. Even
more extensive and significant have been the explorations, by
medicine and the behavorial sciences, of conscience as censor
over instinctual behavior and, as such, a primary cause of
tension. Indeed, it is the conflict between "would" and "should"
in the individual which creates tensions that resolve themselves
in the disguises of neurotic symptoms—in fantasies, in aberrant
behavior, in physical ailments. These findings, based on the
clinical discoveries made by Freud and others have yielded
illuminating insights into the perplexities of human response
to the pressures of industrial living. Without them, we should
hardly have understood cases of individual maladjustment on
the one hand or, on the other, the spectacle of masses escaping
from freedom to "omniscient" Führers and the inappeasable
appetites for power of the leaders themselves.

We may anticipate much more exploration of the impact of
the conscience as censor. But conflicts of this sort are explored
primarily for the light they throw upon pathology in modern
conduct, in behavior at its most extreme—the neuroses and
psychoses of the individual and the psychopathology of politics, war, and totalitarianism in society. If the straightforward
simplicities of "economic man" have thus been lost in the complexities of the convoluted neurotic personality, the "sickness
of the acquisitive society" has also been engulfed in the mortal
perils of power politics!

It is not these abnormal aspects of personality that we are
here exploring in this study of power and morality. We are
dealing, rather, with a very different genre of tensions arising
from the conflicts between the "musts" and the "oughts," the
"woulds" and the "shoulds," of normal human activity. Since
social living is inconceivable without the exercise of power and

since power is itself ethically neutral, the constant direction of power toward beneficent goals is indispensable if it is not to be exploited for evil ends. It is thus essential that conscience continually interpose moral and ethical values as determinants of policy and action. It is not only the immature and neurotic, therefore, but also the mature and stable who confront constant tension, a tension projected by the collision of conscience with the technical imperatives as well as the personal temptations of the workaday world. However well adjusted the homes from which scientists, businessmen, or politicians may come, however conducive preadult experiences may have been to the sound development of personality, there is no escape from the characteristic conflicts of conduct in modern society and from the persisting tensions they engender.

Conscience as embodiment of moral tradition

It is this aspect of the dilemma that we bring up for examination when we insist that conscience as censor is productive of something far more than the abnormal delinquencies and wastelands of our age. For ethical "oughts" are as intrinsic as technical "musts" in the very nature of the responsibilities that must be carried by men to operate American society. Like technical obligations for "good" work, so ethical ideals for the "good" life spring not from Puritan holdovers, but from the very life of the whole social process. Yet, whereas technical tests are externalized and measurable—by quantitative tests in science, figures on productivity in business, or the count of ballots in politics—ethical norms are internal and difficult of measure. They are part of each individual's psychic equipment, derived from his social heritage and transmitted and implanted from one generation to another by such primary insti-

tutions as the family, the church, the school, and the neighborhood.

Sources of American moral tradition

Essentially, this social heritage in America is woven about
three broad interrelated intellectual and spiritual strands: the
religious teachings of Judaic-Christian theology, the humanis-
tic doctrines of Greco-Roman philosophy, and the equalitarian
ideals of our democratic credo.

The Judaic-Christian tradition embodies the most hallowed
and wide-reaching of our moral precepts. The mysteries of
eternal design and of human fate on earth, which sooner or
later preoccupy every one of us, were articulated in sacred
literature long before scientists began to question the extent to
which human conceptual tools can ever give understanding to
the fundamental purpose of the universe.[1] These religious
values—expounded by the Bible and sacred literature and constantly vivified by ceremonial and worship—are implanted in
us from childhood on, values embodying the broadest commandments of personal duty and moral responsibility and encompassing man's relations to his fellows and to God. Even if,
as in some cases, the religious foundation is abandoned, an
ethical residue remains: indeed, religion is often challenged
in its very name. Nevertheless, to do unto others as we would
have done unto us, to succor the widow and orphan, to feed the
hungry and heal the sick, are all impelling motivations stemming from our Judaic-Christian religion.

The second strand, the Greco-Roman tradition, predisposes

[1] Conant, James Bryant, *Modern Science and Modern Man,* Columbia
University Press, New York, 1952, pp. 88–93. Conant, for instance, finds
in *The Book of Job* his own modern resignation to the unknowable in the
problems of good and evil.

us to a life of reason, justice, and beauty. The great ethical literature of Greece, the development of jurisprudence by Rome, the great efflorescence of the Renaissance, the latter-day reemphasis on the breadth of the humanities as against the narrowness of technical and engineering courses—all this is a profound reminder of how earnestly Western civilization, for all its great material success, has sought the way to the moral life.

The third strand, the ideals of an equalitarian democracy, affirms as inalienable the great liberties of mankind and safeguards them from the danger of emasculation by excessive power in the hands of government. In the earlier, simpler days of the sinewy, self-made economic man, this inviolable individual pursued his ends by hard work and frugal living. Amidst the complexities of latter-day society, the same respect for personal dignity finds new expression in protective government activity, in explorations of human relations, and in the philosophies of group organization as sanctions for collective behavior. The democratic credo thus conditions our attitudes and sentiments toward the means and ends of everyday activities with a compelling force superseded only by religion. Indeed, the aspirations implicit in the credo, though predominantly secular, interweave over and again with the beliefs of both the Judaic-Christian and Greco-Roman strands. Where religious counsels, however, tend to be general ("Love thy neighbor") and perfectionist ("Be ye therefore perfect"), and where those of philosophy tend to describe the ideal city or state of man, the counsels of democracy are more explicit and immediately applicable to workaday activities. They have been made vivid for us, moreover, by utterances of national heroes—Washington, Jefferson, Lincoln, the Roosevelts—during critical periods of our history. These documents, like the Gettysburg Address, become hallowed in time and take on a high emotional coloring as they are transmitted through school and community to our children as they grow up into citizenship.

The inalienable rights affirmed in the very act of launching our national independence—every man's right to life, liberty, and the pursuit of happiness—lie deep in our value system. The bills of rights appended to state and Federal constitutions at the birth of the nation further stake out the freedoms that must be kept inviolable: freedom of press, petition, assembly, and worship. All these are outside the reach of power, as is the due process of law designed to protect even the accused from abusive and capricious treatment. Thus it is that the secular system, while not denying the application of religious truths, proves more directly amenable to daily activity than a more fundamental, transcendent religious system. Indeed, in our society, it is through the secular system of government that the commandments of religion are reinterpreted as the social gospel, so to speak, in the light of the changing circumstances to which men must ever adjust their actual lives.

Nature of moral power

It remains to differentiate the power inherent in the moral and ethical realm from that in science, business, and politics. Is it power at all? The answer that immediately comes to mind is a negative one. For, by our very definitions, this system of values is not embodied, as are those of science, business, and politics, in a chain of organized activities marshaling a distinctive power for use within the whole social process. There is nothing about it of a fixed or institutionalized nature. Moral force is made up, rather, of standards of evaluation diffused throughout society by subtle and continuous education and conditioning. The man of uprightness, rectitude, and conscience is a man of power among us. But it is a power of prestige, not one carrying any implication of physical coercion; it cannot, as is the case in business or politics, threaten to deprive anyone of goods, or services, or the opportunity to carry on the functions essential to normal life. It cannot call strikes, postpone production, or imprison those who disagree.

Indeed, it is part of the American pattern that we are not willing to accord to any religious group the power to compel conformity upon others. Precisely because moral values define the standards for judging conduct, those firmly persuaded of their own convictions can in their self-blindness become the most intolerant rulers of men. The past quarter century, with its wars, slave-labor camps, and cremation chambers, has made vivid the dangers of compulsive "righteousness." With the growing concern over the revelations of mental and emotional disturbance, our generation has been confronted with one more puzzle: the psychopathic personality as the champion of social and moral causes. Because historical experience had driven home this lesson a long time ago, the founders of the Republic wrote into our Constitution as public policy both the guarantee of individual freedom of worship and, even more important, the prohibition of an established church. And, in our own day, we realize anew that a fanatically held political faith can generate the same degree of intolerance and cruelty as the zealots of another age who proclaimed their church and their followers as the only true and elect, justifying inquisitions and torture if need be to save the heretics from eternal damnation.

Conscience strongest of powers, though without physical sanctions

Conscience, therefore, though constantly challenging men's conduct in daily work and living, is in America powerless in the sense of direct coercion. Yet, in another and more pervasive sense, it is implacable. Man is constantly tortured as he attempts to make peace with himself in terms of ethical conduct. "Man feels he must always give account of himself to himself." To be sure, this ceaseless effort generates much moralizing, as well as true morality, and many pseudo justifications for self-interest, as well as genuine responsibility for the general welfare, a duality that demonstrates that the power of conscience too, like all other power, contains its amoral potential. But, again, let us not pause to bewail the hypocrites in our midst, any more than to diagnose the psychopaths, serious as in all truth these two groups are in their amoral perversion of power for self-gratification.

Let us, instead, stay with the normal, the mature, with those who seek a responsible course of action. It is the tensions these men experience, the intrinsic conflict between the technical "must" and the ethical "ought," which demonstrate how deeply rooted are the moral imperatives implanted in the typical child within his normal community. Strangely enough, the institutions transmitting these moral values to our youth are the least coercive—the family, the church, the school, the neighborhood —they exert no powers of compulsion or duress comparable to those wielded by the corporation, the union, and, certainly, the government. Yet conscience has forced men to do strange things. It has caused a Jeremiah to denounce his society, a Martin Luther to persecute in the name of the true faith. Moreover, our very tolerance of the faith of others who do not agree with us, our very freedom to express dissenting opinion in the market place of ideas—the measure of our concept of justice and liberty—instead of freeing us from tensions, serve only to sharpen them. For the businessman or the government official is always being challenged by the opposition in terms of the very moral code by means of which he professes to live. Finally, because each of us is his own most relentless censor, the tensions become all the more acute, all the more insistent and omnipresent, as we go about the business of making decisions as to the most effective way of discharging our responsibilities from day to day in whatever role we may find ourselves, as businessmen, labor leaders, government officials or scientists— decisions which involve the use of power in opposing others who are also acting morally according to their conscience.

Thus, as we reach the end of the first part of this exploration into the moral dilemma posed by the technical "must" versus the ethical "ought," we find that scientific, business, and political powers are essential, diverse, and growing in modern industrial society, but that they are also saturated with moral implications from the outset. We find that moral power is devoid of coercive power, and seemingly the most powerless among the forces shaping our normal activities. Yet, in a subtle sense, morality, in the form of conscience, is the most compelling of all powers in the individual who wields power. And it is in the name of moral duty, rather than that of business, science, or politics, that men rebuild bombed cities, rehabilitate nations, and extend ever increasing help and hope to the underprivileged in the world.

But conscience alone not enough as tamer of power

This is as it should be. For the prime function of conscience as power is to direct man's energy toward ethical and spiritual goals. The fact that tensions arise at all when one makes practical everyday decisions in business, politics, or technology is itself dramatic evidence of the unique power of moral values. But, since every man is so often in an ambiguous position between his self-interest and the interest of the whole community, and since whatever guides he has for resolving the conflict between the technical "must" and the ethical "ought" are at best vague and unspecified, we must turn now to the exploration of other measures for stabilizing and taming power. The moral system can at best offer only the seedbed for responsible, ethical behavior. Other forces must be found which, implemented by moral values, may turn power from harmful into beneficent channels.

part two

THE TAMING OF POWER

8. *Reason as tamer of power*

Where to turn for ways of controlling our great man-made powers and how to guide and harness them to human purposes present no simple problem. Indeed, if power itself is amoral, how are we to find ways of controlling the destructive aspects of scientific, economic, and political power and at the same time strengthen the creative pull of moral power toward the good life?

Indeed, is *control* actually what we are looking for? For control implies the delegation of power to some men over other or all men; yet all historic experience warns that such delegation sharpens the appetite for more power. Control imparts further a Frankenstein quality to the direction of power, implying that it is something to be manipulated and exploited. It is precisely experience of this sort that has led generation after generation to fear power as dominantly evil. It was not merely clever phrasemaking but rather bitter experience that impelled history to stamp a coin with the image of Niccolo Machiavelli, a coin which symbolized ". . . his surname . . . [as] an epithet for a knave, and . . . Christian name a synonyme for the Devil."[1]

It is only recently, however, that men's power over nature has become great enough to need explicit control. It is true that the evils multiplied with the good during the nineteenth century with the rise of science and technology and the resultant increased flow of goods and services. If there were now these beneficent results, they were accompanied also by dislocations, child and women's labor, punitive approaches to the destitute under the poor law, sharp inequalities in wealth, unemployment, and dependence on a job for one's livelihood. Yet, as we look back now, however much we may be moved by the miseries to which men were subject during the transition, we also see that these new powers were truly ushering in an industrial revolution which promised a fuller life in at least a material sense. The revolution in industrial technology and the contemporaneous political revolutions promised to free men from old tyrannies and deprivations, natural as well as man-made.

But, as these powers in turn attain maturity, we are rediscovering in the middle of the twentieth century that they too, for all their continuing potential for good, are still amoral. Indeed, the evils locked in modern power attain dimensions more alarming than in any previous period of history. If the hydrogen bomb symbolizes most vividly the ominous shape in which the age-old problems of power reappear, it also thereby confronts modern man most inescapably with the urgency of human *controls.*

[1] Thomas B. Macaulay on Niccolo Machiavelli in *Critical, Historical and Miscellaneous Essays* (New York, 1860) as quoted by Ernst Cassirer in *The Myth of the State*, New Haven, Yale University Press, 1946, pp. 116–117.

Yet the word *control* raises its warning echoes from so many Gethsemanes of the past. A quest for control may mark a turning back on tracks we had well left behind. Men of affairs everywhere, at the threshold of our modern age, anticipated an automatic beneficence, an inevitable progress growing out of science, reason, and democracy. Controls, they felt sure, could be held to a bare safe minimum. Men, endowed with innate capacity for rational thinking and moral discrimination, needed only fair and equal opportunities to make choices and contributions adding up to the greatest good for the greatest number. This is not the place to dwell once more upon the disappointments with this view. What rather emerges as pertinent is its counterpart—the widespread and profound skepticism that has shaken our fundamental confidence in inevitable progress, in the automatically beneficent dynamic forces underlying science and modern industrial society.

Nor is an answer to be found in polar opposites. The tendency to make extreme swings under disillusion is natural. Has laissez faire contained a false prescription? Then let us retreat from reason! Has science produced the hydrogen bomb? Then let us declare a moratorium on science!

But, before despairing, we should ask whether still other ways may not lie open. We do not easily solve the new difficulties arising from the use of scientific, industrial, or political power by invoking the old evils from which we slowly found our measure of freedom. Certainly there is nothing new in vesting control in some men because of birth, conquest, party, or religion and thereby giving them authority to decide what other men must do or think or say or hear. If modern totalitarian rulers seem of a different order from the historic despots, it is only because they wield instruments of modern technology in a world narrowed and telescoped by these same tools. The ruling of men's minds through the newer instruments of communication is only a step away from the imprisonment of their bodies. But, if it is the state which has grasped these functions of central planning and decision, experience reveals that no institution, public or private, may safely be given unchecked the reins of control. Just as the absolute state has come to mean the political officials, whether the party politicians, or the army generals, or the chiefs of police, or perhaps an uneasy alliance among these agents of coercion, just so laissez faire, with lack of any central guidance, means that the balance of power rests on the side of those who already possess economic power in the social structure. Thus, from the beginning up to the 1930s, during the long period of industrial expansion, business was in the saddle. We then came to fear and question the unrestrained sway of industry–as, more recently, the first power thrust of organized labor.

Taming—not control—the more feasible approach

When we move, therefore, from exploring the character of power into the questions of how to achieve its beneficent use, we seem merely to deepen the dilemma. We cannot leave matters to minimum controls; nor can we find a safe channel for administering controls. For control itself implies power–and, in industrial society, an ever growing power. To dig our way out of this seeming impasse, what we really need is, not controls over power, nor a restoration of a system of no control or little control, nor a still longer leap back for central controls in the hands of any sovereign authority, but a way of *taming* power, of domesticating it, through the action of people themselves as individuals and groups, within the bounds of an ordered and orderly society. The taming of power thus requires something both more and less than its control, something between the minimal regulations and obvious inadequacies of laissez faire and the maximum encroachments and continuous overload of central controls.

Reason as tamer

Nor are we likely to find solutions in any magical or miraculous devices outside man and his society. Man creates power. It is in man that the power systems find their natural habitat. And it is man who must learn how to use power without destroying himself. Let us reexamine, then, some of the ways available to us—ways that have always been at our hand, and which, indeed, have been utilized in whatever progress we have thus far made.

We begin by reassessing reason—the major traditional method we have used for problem solving. Our forebears rated high men's capacity to reason amidst the pressures of everyday living. Though they hailed this component in man's endowment, they were not blind to the sway of human passions, prejudices, and special interests. They linked reason, therefore, with the equally basic human endowment for morality. Reason offered a peculiarly human tool of control, which would lead men in the right directions with means sanctioned by acceptable standards of fitness.

Why do we, then, in our own day place so much less reliance on reason? Is it that the potentialities of our present powers are so dangerous, the dilemma so complex, and the available choices so uncertain that human reason looms frail and inadequate in comparison? Or do we look to reason for too total an answer, seeing it as the only solution rather than one among several? In other words, is our very misconception concern-

ing the proper role of reason—the role it always has served and
continues now to serve—one more clue we must explore? Where,
how much, and by what evidence does reason leave the marks
of its influence? What demonstrable role can we establish for
reason, and, obversely, where must reason leave off in the business of taming power?

Reason in science and technology

When we turn to science and technology, it seems almost
superfluous to raise any question concerning the place of reason. Surely science, pure or applied, physical or social, constitutes preeminently the domain of reason. Indeed, so paradoxical is it to admit any retreat from reason in this area that ex-
planations are offered to bypass the paradox. Thus, it may be
conceded that the domain of science constitutes a sovereign
realm of reason, *but* the sciences of man are said to lag dan-
gerously behind the natural sciences! Or science as applied
reason may yield great technical masteries, *but* man's suscep-
tibility to sin renders these masteries a dangerous temptation.
Whether, then, the fault lies primarily in modern science itself
or in frail and sinful man, the decline of reason is proclaimed
even in an age of science.

The difficulty in this regard lies in a failure to recognize that,
while the essential techniques of science and technology are
dominated by reason, that does not mean that the method employed in the physical sciences exhausts all types of rational
thinking, or that there is one, and only one, method of scientific study. Yet such a notion has percolated into the thought
streams of our times—quite understandably—for the very prestige, the very dimensions of the accomplishments in science
have made it natural to identify the methods of *natural* or

physical science as the principal if not the only form of rational, logical thinking. The method of natural science, however, constitutes one and only one species, as it were, of human reason—the most rigorous, organized, and systematic formulation, true, but still only one system through which reason operates. The fact that the social sciences are not easily subject to the same quantitative test as is physical science does not mean that they are not rational. Our modern age has forgotten that reason itself meant different things to Thomas Aquinas, Spinoza, and Newton—rationalists all! Even within the natural sciences, moreover, no single pattern of observation and measurement, of experiments and controls, seems to offer a uniformly applicable method for study. Neither astronomy nor geology, for instance, can utilize control experiments. Each separate field of inquiry, therefore, may have to make whatever adjustments of method are necessary to fit the varying requirements of the materials under study.

If the fields within the natural sciences themselves require specifically adjusted methods of logical thinking, certainly business and politics will find it necessary to make their own adjustments of rational and logical thinking to their characteristic content. In its broadest connotations, the rational approach simply projects a deliberate, systematic, and evaluated adjustment of available means to the promotion of recognized objectives, and, thus, by its very nature, must vary as it is applied to the distinctive content of organized workaday activities. Indeed, so specific are the materials upon which reason is exercised that scientific disciplines simply set the outside limits for rationality, rather than a uniform model.

Just as reason may take on a variety of specific methods in the various fields of science, just so reason is a major influence, through science, in man's attempt to transcend time. Thus, for the layman, science encompasses a concrete aggregate of material marvels, television, motorcars, antibiotics, atom and hydrogen bombs, and so on, seemingly ad infinitum. But, for the scientist, science furnishes a different accumulation: it builds the stockpile of theory and technical knowledge itself. This stockpile, in its turn, conditions behavior along rational lines, furnishing the base of logical thought and scientific construction from which each generation of scientists "takes off" on its own investigations. These, in turn, furnish the base for future scientists—and so on, in an endless accumulation of advancing knowledge.

How, then, with research thus envisaged as a basic link in the chain of organized activity constituting our workaday society, can reason be surrendered or dismissed by any conceivable indictment in our age of science? If it be said that reason serves mainly to make discovery and invention more fruitful, and thus increase the dimension of power without facing up to its moral implications, then two answers may be given. To the extent that science has as its objective the most rigorous search for truth, it vivifies one of the strongest moral virtues. Truth is, and always has been, man's only weapon against darkness. Again, it offers a model for methods of investigation that, with appropriate modifications, may be adapted to the scientific study of man in his multiple relationships. It is only within recent years that funds have been made available for a real attempt to understand human behavior. In all likelihood a considerable period of time may have to pass before we accumulate enough findings to enable us to project methods whereby power can be subordinated to the direction of mind and spirit. Again, the systematic study of such institutions as corporations, governments, and unions may give us a new approach to the administrative process by means of which these power systems can best be governed. For it is industry and government, rather than science, which confront the major moral dilemma in the use of power. The fundamental question, therefore, becomes: To what extent can reason help tame power in business and in politics?

Reason and business

While not to the same degree, it is dangerous in business as in science to envisage any abdication of reason. To be sure, modern industry is continuously involved with intractable, unpredictable human individuals, both as agents in the work environment and as consumers in the open market. But this fact does not diminish essential reliances upon reason; rather, as already indicated, it alters methods as compared with those in the physical sciences.

The difference emerges in clearest outline when we recall that logical thinking generally projects deliberate and systematic adjustment of evaluated means to defined ends. In science, discovery itself is the end. The essence of the method is to follow unfolding facts and observations wherever they may lead. In business, however, the objective is explicitly defined. As Max Weber pointed out some time ago, modern capitalism constitutes the first *rationalistic* economic system, in which means are continuously and consciously fitted to attain a profit.[1] This necessity must not lead us to attribute to "the moving spirits of modern capitalism . . . a stronger economic impulse than, for example, an Oriental trader" possesses.[2] Such notions of relative acquisitiveness are childish. It is the

[1] Weber, Max, *The Protestant Ethic and the Spirit of Capitalism*, translated by Talcott Parsons; New York, Charles Scribner's Sons, 1952, pp. 67–68; first published in Great Britain in 1930.

[2] Idem, *General Economic History*, translated by Frank H. Knight; London, George Allen & Unwin, Ltd., 1923, pp. 355–356.

rationalism of capitalist economic activity that gives our
economy its distinctive place in human history.

As circumstances change, moreover, so do the means in
reaching the broad objective of producing goods and yielding
thereby "the most important criterion . . . private profitable-
ness."[1] For profit as a test of effective management remains a
residual measure, a quantitative figure, expressing the difference between total costs and total receipts. These items vary,
however, not only with market conditions and managerial ability, but also with communal standards of fair wages, conditions
of work, quality of ware, social security, as well as the power
of the group to enforce claims above statutory or competitive
minimal standards. When this happens, the manager must
bring an ever more rigorous quality of rational thinking to his
evolving job content as he is compelled to mobilize capital, materials, labor, plant, and whatever other factors are essential
to the ends of producing goods for the community and of yielding profit to his own institution. For now his control of the elements of his job is circumscribed within "floors" and "ceil-
ings" upon operating costs and distributive claims; these become the most challenging elements of his job. Nor can he rely
even upon these measures of effectiveness—costs, productivity,
and profits—as securely as the natural scientist can upon verification of his results by other investigators. Yet, since the enterprise must remain solvent to stay in business, decisions
must in the final analysis be conditioned by tests of the balance
sheet.

A manager may shut down or move a plant that has been
showing persisting losses; but, by meeting thus the rational
test of profitability, he embarks upon action that raises, as we

---

[1] Idem, *The Protestant Ethic and the Spirit of Capitalism*, p. 162.

have seen, human and social and, therefore, moral issues. The rational tests themselves, in other words, call for recurring re-appraisals, just as do the component means and ends of business logic.

The closer the activities lie to the technical domain of natural science—chemistry, physics, mechanics, engineering, as embodied in production and factory layout—the more rigorously can the materials be subjected to the rational procedures of scientific method. Automation, for instance, is only the latest application of logic to the productive process, an impersonal logic, indeed, in which the controls and directional forces to run a factory can be put on tape, which in turn starts and stops machines in physically optimum cycles. As management moves, however, toward areas where human choices and motivations play an increasing role, rigorous engineering procedures must be modified or may not even be available. And, while it is true that, even in science, logical thinking must be adapted to characteristic materials, the adjustments demanded of the business administrator impose difficulties beyond any which the scientist must face.

When men appear before him as employees and staff members, as purchasers of his products, or as stockholders, the business administrator must view them not only technically, as does the scientist, but also politically and ethically, psychologically and socially, as does a teacher, minister, or physician. Consider, for example, problems arising in the area of production. The effort to apply such rational measures as time and motion study in order to set standards of output and incentive rates stemmed from engineering approaches to the technical problems of production. The long resistance these procedures evoked grew out of multiple causes, partly abuses by management and partly the natural resentment against techniques that seemed to reduce individuals to impersonal factors of production. Yet, by the middle of this century, unions, in a reversal of their earlier role, widely accepted variants of time and motion study. Human consent and participation had been established. In Russia, the correlated aspects of incentive systems and production standards had been manipulated at the same time into the propagandist ballyhoo of Stakhanovism. Examples of shop humor leaking out of Russian and satellite factories, however, raise questions as to the extent to which suspicion of the "speed-up" had really been allayed. The difference in the United States is that the introduction of technical devices for readjusting work and wages had been undergoing modifications by three new currents: the growing professionalism of business management, with emphasis on reasonable uses of scientific method compatible with fair rewards by some mutually agreed upon standard; the political safeguards negotiated with unions to prevent abuse and so create at least a favorable attitude in the shop toward increased productivity; and the developing behavioral or social sciences under the rubric of human relations which deal with motivation both in individual and group expression. In other words, here is an example of scientific method tailored to the unique environment and materials of business.

Patently, here is an example of ways of taming the powers potential in advancing industrialization, at the points where workaday administration raises issues of dislocations and inequities. These devices all represent, moreover, efforts to impose rational "due-process" controls upon procedures by which technical power is marshaled and maximized.

Let us scrutinize for a moment the intrinsic, rational character of these taming devices and their impact upon the power of business, as compared to that of science and technology. In both areas, job performance proves to be a series of methods, each adapted to the specific materials, from the physical and engineering sciences to the human and social sciences. To the scientist, however, no matter what adjustments to materials may be necessary his responsibility remains unchanged. As scientist, whether studying light, or the atom, or the stars, or man, he applies the tests of logic to establish the validity of his findings. The powers that his laboratory ultimately makes available to the community involve no moral issues for him as scientist. If their amorality, with the potential for evil, comes to appall him, he confronts that moral issue as an individual technically more qualified to speak on the nature of the new power than his fellow citizens but no more morally responsible. As an individual, he can vow, as some have, that he personally will no longer engage in research directed toward new instruments of war. But so long as he does collaborate in making new discoveries which lead to deadlier weapons, he can make no individual decision concerning the uses of his findings.

The case is sharply different with the business executive. The powers from his universe, as already pointed out, are immediately of a twofold nature. He mobilizes for society a power for satisfying wants through an organized system of highly complex, interdependent, technical, and human activities. But in mobilizing that power, he must, as we have seen, make continuous decisions that involve the exercise of power over other men. This power is so enmeshed in the technical necessities of efficiency that few businessmen recognize that they are wielders of power. On the other side, critics of business see little more than the abuse of this power over other men—in layoffs of workers, adjustments of wages and prices, relocations of plants, resistance to social legislation, monopoly prices to consumers, and so forth. And, because a major test of effective performance is profitability, not to say solvency, decision making has long involved the businessman in moral-technical ambiguities and defensiveness in a world in which he is operating most of the time under unfriendly, if not hostile, scrutiny.

The executive's available adjustments, moreover, vary sharply from those of the scientist. Though he is endlessly involved with people as superiors, as subordinates, as bench and office forces, as suppliers, as buyers, as union representatives, as government agents, and so endlessly round the job circle, he cannot postpone issues of moral and social responsibility until technical objectives of turning out goods and services have been attained. Nor can he make decisions purely in terms of accepted technical criteria; these decisions impinge immediately and variously on the actual lives of other men and so raise questions of authority and consent. Indeed, the moral challenge for the manager is much more complex than for the scientist. The latter shares his profound moral disturbance as a common burden with his fellow citizens; but the industrial manager carries a moral burden which he cannot share. It is not only that he must make decisions which may have harmful consequences; he must make decisions the consequences of which he does not even fully know. The decision he makes to promote, for example, the productivity of synthetic fibers may create grave dislocations in the manufacture of natural fiber. Business procedures, moreover, unlike those of science, are influenced by self-interest as well as by technical requirements. The manager's own job and his own remuneration, the return to the owners he represents, and the solvency of the business are safeguarded by technical decisions, but these may also result in laying off workers or creating ghost towns. In the long run, the community may also gain, but the merits of one decision against another contain ambiguous counters of interest.

As a check on the manager's self-interest, organizations arise to challenge him; and so one more element is added to his job, that of handling the strong voices raised against him and the alternative measures they propose.

The identity between the moral concern of the scientist and that of the layman concerned with the potential for evil in nuclear fission, which begins when the scientist's daily work is over, finds only a blurred counterpart in the world of business. Generally we agree on the end goals of productivity and an ever higher standard of living. It is the day-to-day decisions, rather than the goals themselves, which in business give rise to the most critical of moral conflicts. Thus it is that management inevitably must make adjustments involving rational thinking and specialized techniques. The handling of materials, plant layout, and engineering aspects in general call for the rationalism typical of applied scientific method. These aspects thus create little new challenge. But the handling of human beings, as individuals and as groups, does raise questions of use–and of moral implication. Since men as employees are factors of production, and therefore of cost, shall insights into human motivation be utilized to exploit men as so many malleable cost factors? Or shall these insights be utilized in the effort to obtain participation and consensus for what are deemed technically sound programs? Even if such be the end, how can any manager be certain that his own self-interest may not get in the way? Even after the initial power tug with interest groups has been settled, and the new rights of protest and the review of decisions established, technical needs still may compel decisions carrying adverse human consequences. While the economic administrator still retains the power to make such decisions, the changing standards of social responsibility call for ever new answers. Alleviations for layoffs, for technological displacements, and for irregular work, may be provided—and, within limits, often are—in the individual enterprise. But comprehensive government programs are more likely to be called for.

The executive accordingly must not only assimilate the technical aspects of his job but also safeguard his own power of decision making, as well as handle power relations with other interest groups and the expanding role of government. The fact that the tests of technical performance are neither as clean-cut as their quantitative format would lead us to expect, nor as accepted by the community as are the criteria available to science, does not simplify his task. And, yet, the ever growing complexity of the job calls more and more for rational, logical thinking and procedures.

How to meet this need, both in its logical aspects—the materials and machinery necessary for production—and in its nonlogical, human aspects, is reflected in the ferment going on in the world of education and business. Hardly a university but harbors a center of human or industrial relations, with emphasis on research in the behavioral sciences. Both the theoretical aspects and insights gained from field studies in factory, store, and community are being studied. A literature is accumulating. Similarly, corporations are developing programs of executive training, sometimes in the plant itself, sometimes in university environments, sometimes in both. Here again it is the nonlogical, human factor which receives the emphasis.

Because of the lack as yet of a substantive core of principles and procedures, the case method has become a primary tool for exposing students empirically to the experience and logic of industry. The case method enables the instructor and the student to view typical problems that face business, in all their manifold technical, social, and political ramifications. The aim is to build a rational, responsible approach upon the method that has so far been most effective in mobilizing the facts of a given situation—both logical and nonlogical—in a dynamic framework of action.

Indeed, without a foundation in rational organization, our centers of production would be impossible dreams. To move through a motor plant, a steel mill, or an oil refinery is to be struck by the systematic activities that unite so many hundreds of men at varying, segmented tasks to move parts toward an assembled finished product. Beyond all the pulling and hauling, beyond the daily frictions, large and small, the wheels go round with the clock, the raw materials go in from the mines and the forest and the earth and the seas, and the end products emerge for distribution to consumer markets. The regularities, the rhythm, the cooperation, may be imposed, and men to some degree may chafe under supervision, even as they relish the cooperativeness and its results. But from Biblical days on, men have chafed as they toiled. Previously, however, before the advent of technology, it was the rhythms of nature that imposed the major disciplines and regularities. As children of nature themselves, men may have found the work routines of the land and the sea perhaps less overwhelming; but, significantly, they were clothed in ritual and magic to be rendered more acceptable. With the rise of modern industry, on the other hand, new problems of managing men have emerged. Power and counterpower, traditional codes and new moral responsibilities, established disciplines and rational readjustment to changing conditions, have all gradually transformed and complicated the job of procuring sustenance and satisfactions. These very complications, in turn, have called for cooperative interdependence and technological efficiency, which could not be maintained without rational thought and planning. Reason has thus not only helped to enlarge the power of industry but has also led to the development of new scientific approaches to the problem of understanding and integrating nonlogical human behavior into this interdependent system of production.

And this emphasis on a scientific approach to human factors is in its very beginning. Already substantial gains have accrued to managerial personnel—to say nothing of new findings which have deepened the insights of economists, psychologists, political scientists, sociologists, and anthropologists. The older democratic concept of a "voice in government" has been adapted to industry, so as to assure greater participation in decision making on the part of staff and employees at all levels. The problem of communications in such a complex institution as a corporation has been and is continuing to receive close study and experimentation. The supervisor now realizes that it is just as important "to listen" as it is "to tell." The establishment of discipline has become a complex exercise in administering authority with consent and under due process. It is accepted increasingly that human beings are to a large extent self-directive and seek satisfactions in group life in the factory as they do in the outside community. The list might be multiplied. Indeed, anyone now in his late middle years who contrasts his current experience in industry with what took place in the first twenty-five years of this century, cannot help being impressed by the dramatic contrast in the way the typical shop is managed. Foremen and superintendents just don't seem to be the same type of human beings. Presidents and chief executives are concerned with the latest developments in human relations. Men are given time off to study and confer on the best methods of securing maximum cooperation (not obedience!) from the men assigned to them. In the old days, a worker who dared disobey was given—in the words of industry—the "bum's rush" as he was escorted to the gate. Nowadays, he will be encouraged to talk about his difficulty, to express what is "blocking" him. He may in some companies, indeed, end up in the office of a therapist!

Compared to the rigid methodology of the physical scientist's laboratory, all these developments in business are as yet in quite a crude stage. It will take time to experiment and devise methods of identifying strategic factors in human behavior. But the significant thing to be noted is that a real beginning has been made. Thus, in business no more than in science does reason have to abdicate. Indeed, the very logic of events has propelled industry to turn more and more to the scientific method as a way of discovering how to exercise power with a greater degree of human effectiveness and responsibility.

Reason as tamer of power: constitutionalism

The greatest contribution reason makes to the taming of power in government is in the development of constitutionalism. For constitutionalism is nothing but embodied rationality —reason applied to the structure, distribution, and limits of power vested in elected or appointed officials. Thus, democratic government is founded upon a fundamental structure of sanctioned procedures for resolving differences by the rule of reason—a system of law and order, a continuously evolving historic constitutionalism. By its very genesis, constitutionalism projects a taming of power. The adoption of the Constitution of the United States, the earlier wresting of the Magna Charta from King John, the slow cumulation of common law—these define and limit the most absolute powers any men can wield over their fellows—over life, liberty, property, welfare, and happiness. Accordingly, political history contains its never ending record of men's struggles to modify or limit the arbitrary and capricious use of power, and to put it in an orderly and defined framework.

The Federal principle embodied in our Constitution is an excellent illustration of the structuring of power: the compromises between large and small states in representative national councils, between old established states and those still to be carved out of virgin lands; the enumeration of responsibilities to be discharged by government; the rights to be reserved and safeguarded to individuals; the powers denied to the several states and the national government, to church or judiciary, to police or military; and the divisions of power between executive, legislative, and judiciary. The men who drafted our Constitution gave due consideration to conflicting as well as common interests, and therefore foresaw the role as well as the dangers of power. Accordingly, they studied how best to check any concentration of power in the hands of any one interest, party, or institution.

Thus it is that constitutionalism embodies a rational procedure for tempering the power of interest blocs and economic groups. These blocs exert pressures for favorable platform planks in election campaigns and, after elections, for political appointments and favorable legislation. When all the pros and cons have been heard and debated and the last compromise incorporated, the final test lies in a count of the yeas and the nays. Thus majority rule represents a built-in, agreed-upon procedure for registering changing shifts in the balance of power. Enactment of law, however, begins, rather than ends, the process. Experience with any legislation becomes the data for subsequent efforts at revision; conflicts raise issues which are carried through the judicial network. Yet even members of

the Supreme Court may not be unanimous on the question of
the constitutionality of a particular legislative or executive
action: cases settled by a majority of one are by no means un-
common. In time, therefore, with new court appointments, a
minority opinion of one era may well become a majority
opinion of another. A final recourse remains open–that of constitutional amendment by a majority of three-quarters of the
states. Constitutionalism thus represents once more an adapta-
tion of the methods of reason to nothing less than conflicts or
differences over the uses of power for political, economic, and
social ends.

This same form of constitutionalism is embedded in the
power structure of industry, as defined both in trade-union
agreements and in legislation. As organized labor achieves
power, it gradually limits through collective bargaining the
one-sided exercise of economic power by employers. The right
to discharge–the chief economic weapon of management–becomes hedged in with a pervasive system of due process, as is,
gradually, the right of promotion and demotion. Collective
bargaining is legalized and, indeed, made mandatory to assure
equality of power between the employees and the corporation.
Here, too, we find that this system of industrial constitutionalism is constantly being debated and modified to make it workable. In addition, laws are replaced or amended so that individual employees may be protected from the danger of excessive
power of union officials as well as of management. Taft-Hartley, for instance, is an attempt to rectify the imbalance arising
out of experience with the Wagner Act.

In the final analysis, of course, conflicts can be brought
within the rational procedures of constitutionalism because
reasonableness itself is part and parcel of the values by which
men live and act in our society. Justice, due process, majority

rule, together with protection of individual and minority rights
—these are all at the very heart of the American credo. To act in
ways and for purposes that commend themselves to one's fellows as fair and reasonable constitutes one of our most pervasive sentiments. The appeal to reason *and* human dignity
explains the continual attempt on the part of those who possess
authority to justify themselves to the electorate that they are
acting not in an arbitrary or capricious manner but always
under the powers granted them in the Constitution to advance
the public weal.

Politics and government

What we have just said about reason as tamer of power
in government gives a somewhat different perspective to the
discussion of political power as analyzed in Chapter VI. For,
clearly, politics as an activity must be distinguished from
government as an administrative process. Politics deals with
the acquisition of power; government, with the administration
of power. In the acquisition of power, reason gives way to emotionalism, to distortion, to amoral and, at times, even immoral
behavior on the part of politicians. Once in office, however,
the same politicians become inevitably surrounded with the
atmosphere as well as the procedures of reason and morality.

If we follow this distinction, it may help us to acquire a
saner, less disturbed attitude. For, in the alarums that are
constantly sounded about the dangers of statism, it is forgotten that the dangerous trends have appeared, not in the
United States, nor in the Anglo-Saxon countries, nor in Western
Europe, but mainly in Central and Eastern Europe. It is true
that, in the upheavals of the twentieth century, it is the state
which has intervened to give statutory mandate to the new

moral responsibilities for security and welfare. Yet, it is forgotten that in this country, as in most of the Western democracies, the approach to the welfare state has been one of gradualism, accompanied by protracted debates on the part of citizens as well as of parties and legislatures—debates based upon laborious investigations into the facts of poverty, involuntary unemployment, and other social problems. It is true, of course, that final embodiment in accepted law has come as the inevitable result of a shift of power from employers and businessmen to labor and farmers. It is equally true that the shift in the United States came in an era of global revolution and counterrevolution that ominously revealed the nonrational components in political behavior and the potential of government for totalitarian evil in achieving controls over a technological economy.

Yet, while we do well to scrutinize such dangers, we need to remember that government must have the authority necessary to provide what is beyond the reach of individual enterprise. An industrial society apparently cannot live effectively without political intervention, even if it is hard to live safely with it. And, if we inquire why this is so, we see clearly that rational approaches are less available in politics than in government or in business management and, of course, much less than in science; for, to the political leader, in contrast with the manager or scientist, the major objective is nothing other than power itself. He must first win the right to run, then secure the votes that give him the power of office, then maintain himself in it by satisfying his electorate, then make firm his position in the party hierarchy, and finally achieve the wider public notice and approval necessary to strengthen his hold on the power that office confers.

The electorate from whom the politician procures his mandate has expanded markedly with the extension of suffrage. The quality of rational argument directed at the voters, however, can hardly be held to have improved–or deteriorated–in any marked degree. The recriminations, vituperations, charges, and countercharges of present-day electioneering find echoing parallels from the campaigns and criticisms directed against Washington, Jefferson, Jackson, Lincoln, and so on down the historic line. From the start, the pages of our history have been dotted with tumult and shouting, as well as deliberation and hard thinking, on the part of statesmen as well as demagogues. Since the decisions of the electorate are thus based upon an admixture of rational argument and emotional response, interest groups have naturally greatly multiplied. For one thing, although political parties are not provided for in the written Constitution, they have arisen as a continuing mechanism. These oligarchial organizations have created, as we have discussed previously, their own ethical problems, often bringing to the hustings not only amoral but even immoral aspects of behavior. The parties serve, however, important positive needs. The two-party system encompasses so wide-ranging a miscellany of interests–regional, economic, class, racial, and religious–that it is salutary to recall how traditionally it has tamed the sharp disunities of splinter factions and proved able to maintain coalitions and workable balances of power.

The further intervention between voter and official of a wide variety of interest associations is another disturbing institution in our large-scale society; for each of these associations constitutes a political entity, with officials appealing to emotions as well as reason and often attaining a continuity in office closer to that of the political boss than that of the elected governmental official. But the internal relationships and activities of organized farmers, labor, retailers, manufacturers, physicians, lawyers, scientists, engineers, and so on through multiple ramifications, all reflect to a larger or smaller degree the stamp of political behavior. Dealings across group lines, in turn, are cast, as we shall see later, in patterns of negotiation or bargaining toward the formulation of compromise, agreement, settlements.

Again, if rational thinking in politics, whatever its channeling, appears today eclipsed by emotional appeals, special pleading, and oversimplifications of forensic conflict, may not all this register the sheer din of modern amplified communication rather than deterioration? The billingsgate of political battle of a century or more ago did not flash across continents through headlines, broadcasts, and television screens. Even today, so long as the audience is not captive, the magnified din can be turned off and quieter voices selected; the cons can be articulated as freely as the pros. And, where this is true, political power retains its built-in checks and correctives—especially when it attains office. The leaders we repudiate may have to await the longer perspectives of history to be seen as statesmen, but at any rate we know that no totalitarian tyrant will rewrite our history sheerly to serve his own immediate self-aggrandizement.

If political debates today, moreover, as 150 years ago, seem to enlist many more attributes than sheer rationality—though reason seldom loses its place completely in the resolution of differences—we must keep in mind the nature of the function that political behavior discharges. For politics, let us recall, unlike science and industry, focuses upon the *distribution* of wealth rather than its creation. Government establishments are not under necessity to follow strict accounting or verifiable facts. Deficits are met by funds raised through taxation. This does not mean that government does not enlist specialized, technical services. On the contrary, this century has witnessed a tremendous multiplication of staff responsibilities and administrative agencies, deeply involved in all the technical implications of science and business. The difficulty comes when differences arise between the staffs of these agencies and the elected officials over issue of power and policy in serving various constituents. Then issues are drawn concerning the uses to which technical knowledge is put and the maintenance of standards of good work regardless of the popularity of results. When the technical issues are clear-cut, the technical staff frequently win over the politicians, even Cabinet members; indeed public officials increasingly protect the competent civil servant against interfering politics. Thus reason exerts its influence; but, at the same time, it remains true that data in the hands of policy makers may implement varying recommendations. This represents neither venality nor a dominating nonrationality, but rather the fact that logic does not always yield a clear-cut answer as to which political approach best serves human ends. Partisans mobilize the pros and cons as they see them. Power does not weigh the scales of decision alone, nor does merit always emerge Minerva-like, full-panoplied from each situation. The assessing of pros and cons, instead, thus emerges as a strategic activity.

It remains for the electorate to exert pressures which, in any given situation, yield the most workable decision. And, if the party in office—and its representatives—unduly offend reason and justice, they are likely to be turned out at the next election. At any rate, the glare of publicity is always focused on those who wield power, and they dare exceed or abuse power—once they operate under the structure of power as defined in the

Constitution—only at the risk of losing all power in the next election.

Reason and morals

It is almost superfluous to inquire into the relation between reason and ethics. Together with aesthetics they go hand in hand from ancient days down to contemporary times. They make up the very heart of the humanist tradition. In a world divided, as ours is, into competitive social systems, we must of necessity turn to reason, logic, and rationalism as the major tools for the evaluation of moral systems by which free people prefer to live. Indeed, the high value put upon reasonableness and justice makes possible the growth and the acceptance of constitutionalism, the submission of the individual to a system of law and order under which all are treated alike, the powerful and the weak, the rich and the poor, the office holder and the man in the ranks.

Here is evident the impact of the Greco-Roman tradition, with its emphasis upon reason and justice and upon the other enduringly large issues of the good life, intermingled with the moral tradition of Judaic-Christian heritage. Yet, in truth, the responsible administrators who must make the daily decisions that keep the wheels of industry and society going must perforce base such decisions on a blend, so to speak, of discipline (that is, power), reason, and ethics. In our complex community we all must live and work under self-imposed cooperation, self-imposed rationality, and self-imposed constitutionalism.

This measure of rational control, innate and inescapable, we are apt to take for granted. But major issues of social justice still remain. By what appeals to reason can we determine whether the very abundance created by American industry is being equitably shared? What standards determine whether a particular rate of profit is justified, whether given prices are just, whether wages are fairly differentiated between the skills of workmen, whether workers are entitled to have pensions, vacation with pay, and minimum annual earnings provided as a fixed cost to business? These ethical issues remain, though they have constituted, since the beginnings of industrial society, the stuff of social and religious discussion.

Can such questions of means and ends be brought within the aegis of reason? Is a science of ethics an achievable objective? Or are these values part of faith and religion; and ethics the residue of the reconciliations men make successively as they differ and collaborate, collaborate and differ, in any generation and from one generation to another? Since moral direction and ethical values have become, through conscience, a major factor in taming power, surely reason cannot now be renounced as a means of discriminating and evaluating the values to be upheld as one faces alternative courses of action within the nation or across national lines.

How, then, in view of the vital function reason plays in such an interdependent social system as that in America, explain the growth of anti-intellectualism in our time? What compels men who have attained a peak strength none imagined possible a century and a half ago to contemplate a retreat from reason, an escape from freedom? Is it possible that the revolt represents fundamentally a rejection of an earlier philosophic misconception concerning the role of reason in modern life—namely, that man would act preeminently upon rational choices, and that, as he made his choices, history would evolve along a straight line of progress?

It cannot be said, as we look back, that the unfolding

achievement of the American people failed completely to justify the hopeful anticipation based upon reason. But the outstanding fruition came in the powers intrinsic in science, technology, and business—in the material aspects of life. Who of us is satisfied that we have achieved the good life, that our spiritual and moral growth is anywhere commensurate with our material success? That is why, though our material powers stand at formidable height, we reassess reason as a tool for directing toward beneficent goals the very power brought forth by reason. And if we find ourselves unable now to rely upon spontaneous generation of rational conduct toward the good life, do we thereby need to renounce reason? Or is it that the fulfillment of human aspiration is a much more difficult struggle than man had anticipated?

9. *Human association as tamer of power*

Human experience, based as it is upon the innermost nature of man, should warn us against relying upon reason alone for the complete job of taming power. For man is also emotional. Though distinguished from other animals for his very capacity to reason, man responds primarily to such drives as fear, anger, love, and to such sentiments as loyalty, hostility, patriotism; but he responds also to reason as a way of checking and directing emotions and sentiments.

Because we prize reason so highly, emotions and sentiments are regarded as obstacles to man's need to adjust to the problems of a complex society. We tend to forget, however, that emotions and sentiments as energizers of action have, like all power, positive as well as negative value in shaping human nature. Indeed, they are responsible for a highly characteristic form of man's behavior—his liking to be with other people. This propensity for association results in various forms of social and political institutions. These in turn constitute a natural vehicle for the taming of power. Because this gregarious drive is universal and innate, causing man everywhere to associate with his fellows in pursuit of his essential purposes, this capacity, like that of reason, is at once a source of powers implementing his capacities for effective living, and a rein for both checking and directing those powers in promoting his ends.

Reason, let us repeat, emerges par excellence as the source of our power over nature, since it constitutes the essential key to the procedures prevailing in science and technology. Thus, reason came to furnish in our age of science the model by which these rational procedures were evaluated in all aspects of industrial society. Granted that the procedures have had to be adjusted to the materials of varying fields of study, it is impossible to conceive of any of our complex business, political, or social institutions without a considerable measure of logical direction and systematic procedure in relation to law, order, and due process. Yet, behind all this rational planning, behind and prior to reason itself, are the basic biological drives—instincts and emotions—and the socially conditioned sentiments, which utilize reason as a tool and are in turn controlled and put under the guidance of reason.

Thus, we find a network of group organizations in the United States today: a crowded, vital, diverse structure of associations, spontaneous as well as planned, fraternal, social, official, quasi-official, voluntary, and governmental. We need not enter here into the specific historical factors that have enriched our national life with this structure of human associations. It is well to remind ourselves, however, that the acceptance of this propensity has from the beginning of our nation made it a recognized source of power as well as a check on power. Interest groups, especially, tend to check one another in the pressures they bring upon other groups and government. The behavior of corporations and unions in their bargaining relationships offers one vivid illustration.

But, if the propensity to form multiple associations may be accepted as firmly rooted in our democratic tradition, the contemporary character giving shape to the phenomenon tends to reflect the problems and dilemmas of our own time. Three major developments deserve attention: (1) new insights into the functioning of spontaneous small groups of men and women—here a social clique, there a political cell or faction; here, again, the heart of the machinery of government, though having only a "kitchen" or backdoor status; (2) a new look at "bigness"—a more discriminating evaluation of the forces generating large-scale enterprise, the usefulness of the enterprise, and the attempt to distribute power within it; (3) the multiplication and expansion of interest organizations—of trade unionists, farmers, professional people, veterans, small businessmen, retailers, wholesalers, and so on—with their pressures and counterpressures on one another and on various agencies of the community, particularly governmental.

The small autonomous group as tamer of power

What is the impact of the small group upon the distribution of power within an enterprise? Does it centralize, or decentralize power? Recent studies have revealed the rise of small unplanned groups around natural leaders within shops, offices, schools, administrative divisions, and, indeed, any place where people come together for any length of time. These groups

seem to form without advance planning on anyone's part. Un-
deniably they satisfy human cravings for fellowship. They
serve as rallying points for a variety of activities, all the way
from horseplay to mutual aid. But—this is significant from a
power viewpoint—they also appear over and again as ways of
resisting new policies. In industry, they slow down technical
innovation, in particular, and shop authority, in general. They
ostracize the pace setter, or as they term him, the "rate buster."
They hold back work to "peg" production records and drag
their feet when under time-study observation. In other words,
they act to all intents and purposes as unrecognized informal
centers of power with a veto on the formal, legal authority of
management. Indeed, frequently they attempt to circumvent
not only managerial authority but also that of their own union
officials and even the grievance machinery provided in the
union agreement. They thereby reveal themselves as intent on
converting the human propensity for association into a checkmate against the power exercised over them in their work
environment.

While the tactics of these small, independent groups may
differ in detail, their reaction to authority is in general a negative one. Thus, the introduction of changes and improvements
in products, methods, or layouts, which require rate revisions,
job reclassifications, or other adjustments in shop organization,
creates situations of conflict all the way from wildcat stoppages
to the pegging of production at the same level for all crews
during the observation period—all this in spite of long-estab-
lished differences in individual abilities. It is not without significance that such practices by these small power groups are
not only of recent vintage but, indeed, antedate the advent of
unions. Thus, Frederick W. Taylor, the founder of scientific
management, describing his first experiments with incentive

systems, vividly describes the threats directed against him by hostile groups of machinists in 1883 upon his appointment as foreman in the Midvale Steel Company. Similar observations are recorded in the wide inquiries made for the Bureau of Labor at the turn of the century under the guidance of John R. Commons.

These small power centers seem best to be described as a sort of industrial underground, interposing checks upon constituted authority. Unlike the underground found in political activities, however, they do not seek to topple legitimate management, though a specific group may now and again have it in for an unpopular foreman, a capricious or arbitrary boss, or even a high-pressure supervisor. Nor do they find it difficult to utilize union loyalties and the grievance machinery for their own ends. Often they compel union officials to "fight" their case through all the grievance machinery, including arbitration, though these officials fully realize the lack of merit in the employees' claims. Covert, yet ingenious, in their strategies of counterpower, they stand forth throughout industry as a persisting underground challenge to established authority.

There is no doubt, then, that these groups serve as a tamer of power, and, like all grass-roots forces, a very effective one. One might wonder, however, what motivates their growth. Is it the revolt of human beings against manipulation by men and against machines, blueprints, policies which are imposed on them? Or is it crude power bargaining to get the greatest returns for the least work on the part of the favored few who belong to the clique? Or does it partake of the nature of outlaw power—the strategic few holding up the many for self-aggrandizement?

Although these cliques are effective in taming power, they are not an unmixed blessing. Like all power holders, they tend to be self-centered and oblivious to the larger good of the community. The blockades they raise against the carrying out of organizational programs, while serving as built-in curbs against arbitrary or capricious decisions, also tend to lower production and undermine necessary discipline. In the extreme form of wildcat stoppages, they introduce a form of anarchy. Indeed, of all the pressure groups existing in this country, these small autonomous cliques constitute the most circumscribed, narrow, and provincial.

And yet it is hard to escape the conclusion that these groups serve a social purpose as a form of counterpower. For one thing, they tend to slow down the rate of introduction of technical decisions, with their concern for efficiency, costs, and profits. Secondly, they slow down authority and, in particular, raise a roadblock against capricious and arbitrary supervision. Their activities, moreover, emerge as a human defense against organizational size in the union as well as in the corporation. Finally, within the group they exercise restraints upon the power drives of individuals who might exploit their fellows as well as company and union for selfish purposes. In a sense, then, they help to socialize the individuals who make up the group and to foster cooperation within it. The group has its own ways of imposing disciplines. While it will frown upon and even ostracize the "rate buster," it will equally under the right shop atmosphere "put the heat" on the shirker who tries to evade his fair share of responsibility and work.

Bigness and decentralization of power

From earliest days, let us recall, we have been perturbed by the threat of bigness: first, of government; then, of business; then, of unions; and, now, of all three. Yet we have also recog-

nized that, whatever the theory, in practice only an organization of considerable size can act effectively on complex, large-
scale problems. We are faced, therefore, not with bigness alone
but, again, with the intrinsic moral dilemma of industrial society. On the one hand, the momentum of power is toward cor-
ruption—corrupting those who wield power as well as those
who curry favor with the wielders. On the other hand, the
equally compelling drift in the technical instruments of industry is toward large-scale organization. The very technology,
moreover, that expands the organizational reach of man's institutions shrinks the physical habitat of interdependent industrial men. But, while it is easy to envisage a technologically
unified world in terms of jets, radio, television, it is difficult to
conceive of a world community under law in terms of the
United Nations.

Human beings are provincial in their sentiments and loyalties to particular nations and regions. They are preoccupied
with the small stuff of everyday living. It therefore is difficult
for people to feel strongly about a large-scale abstraction such
as the United Nations, which comes to life for them only in a
crisis like the Korean war involving their own sons and brothers. Moreover, the sacrifice seems particularly meaningless
and indeed tragic because of the absence of any spontaneous
loyalty to law and order on a global scale.

Within the boundaries of our own nation, we find ourselves
caught in a somewhat different dilemma. For loyalties and
kindred sentiments are already embedded in the people, and
we can count on cooperation with constituted authority in carrying out programs. The dilemma, then, arises out of the need for
large-scale powers to accomplish socially desirable goals. Yet
these powers are dangerous in their threat to freedom. Hence,

the curbs upon the powers we need—though proving ever more large-scale—must be found within and between the organizations which mobilize and administer those powers; yet these curbs must be found in such a way that no organization may gain absolute control.

Thus our fresh look at the problem of bigness must be directed toward discovering what checks are available to limit the potential abuse while preserving power for effective service to the community. Such checks have been developing in three different areas: (1) from within corporate organization itself; (2) from the multiple-interest organizations, which interact both cooperatively and competitively; and (3) from agencies outside industry and government.

One of the most striking movements is the growing trend in business to decentralize authority from corporate headquarters to local operating units, as General Motors and Sears, Roebuck have been doing for some time and, in the last few years, the Ford Motor Company. Here is a tendency contrary to historical experience, experience which reveals the logic of power as tending toward greater and greater concentration. For it is the power wielders in industry who are diminishing the scope of their own authority and delegating it to local managements, to men who are in reality their subordinates! Moreover, all this has been taking place in business during the same period that the political state has evinced an opposite tendency, that of denuding local authority of power and concentrating it more and more in the hands of the national government.

While we can do little more here than record the event, this contradictory drift in business and government deserves thoroughgoing future study. What it means in business is that authority lodged in management for the conduct of an enterprise is by deliberate and formal policy delegated by the top officials at headquarters to lower officials in constituent units of operation. Underlying this move is a basic and growing conviction that an organization may become too large even for efficiency. It is all but impossible for central executives to have at their command both the facts and the "feel" of the local situation and to be able to make effective decisions on problems as they arise from day to day. Moreover, a direct sense of responsibility by staff personnel at local levels mobilizes energy, concern, and conviction that what they do matters. Similarly, decentralization provides richer interpersonal relations at the operating level and therefore more effective channels between customers, foremen, intermediate supervisors, workers, local citizens, and plant managers.

The allocation of power between central and local authority, of course, has constituted a central theme in America from the very day of its founding. In that sense, indeed, our entire nation has constituted a laboratory with a continuous, never ending experiment. In the early years of our history, with the need to provide a strong but democratic central government, the matter of power in government held exclusive attention. Beginning with the latter part of the nineteenth century, business has come under severe criticism. As its leadership has become professionalized and administrative-minded, major priority has been given to the question of what to centralize and what to decentralize. Thus in corporation after corporation we find diverse programs and continuous modifications in the allocating of responsibilities for manufacture and sales, for instance, to the people directly involved in their execution, while reserving to the central authority of the corporation such functions as general over-all policies, finances, and government relations.

Moreover, there is a growing tendency, in contrast to older practice, for large businesses to encourage small competitive businesses, not only because it is good public policy, but also because the latter turn out at less cost some products needed in the final assembly at the larger plant.

In addition to this voluntary distribution of power within the corporation, the power of business, as indicated earlier, is being constantly checked by competitive institutions such as trade unions—witness the growth of collective bargaining in the past twenty-five years. And, obversely, organized labor is kept within bounds of reasonableness and practicability by business. The restraint upon managerial authority exercised by unions through the negotiation and administration of agreements reveals significant uniformities—precisely because the union does impose limits upon the vested powers of management. But it is also true that many diversities appear in the ever evolving joint relationships—diversities both within the same given organization, as time adds to experience and understanding, and within the whole network of collective bargaining. Thus we have indicated elsewhere at least eight patterns of distinctive relationships of this type: (1) conflict; (2) containment-aggression; (3) ideology; (4) power-bargaining; (5) deal-bargaining; (6) collusion; (7) accommodation; and (8) cooperation.[1] Here we can only note that the differentiating characteristics in these patterns of relationships stem from the degree to which power is used in their development, from a maximum in patterns of conflict, containment, and ideology, to a minimum in patterns of accommodation and cooperation.

[1] "Some Implications and Problems of Collective Bargaining," *The New Industrial Relations*, Ithaca, New York, Cornell University Press, 1948, pp. 33–65; and "Varieties of Labor Relations," *Harvard Business Review*, Vol. XXVII, No. 2, March, 1949, pp. 175–199.

Checks and counterchecks as tamers of power

In contrast with the trend in industry, the momentum of power in politics, a momentum toward centralized authority and expanding controls, causes alarm precisely because the power that is thus expanding is potentially the most absolute and dangerous of all powers–sovereign power, with its capacity to deprive the individual of liberty and even of life. It was to avert any such aggrandizement and concentration of power that the founders of our country divided power in our Constitution allocating it to separate agencies. The functions of government since the beginning of the nation, therefore, have been divided among the executive, the legislative, and the judiciary, each with its own demarked orbit, under defined checks and balances. Again, between the states and the Federal government, powers have been specifically and respectively delegated, prohibited, and reserved.

Much of our political history has been devoted to the working out of these basic checks and balances written into the structure of government. These checks and balances have in turn become the targets and the instruments of struggles among economic classes, regional interests, political factions, and pressure groups as they have sought to gain the support of government by influencing the Congress or the President or both. These movements, of course, are colored by the individual men who give leadership to the causes involved in the clashes of power. Strong men inevitably leave their impress upon the shape of events. A strong President not only checks legislative encroachments but also furnishes direction as he responds to the multiplicity of pressures for specific legislation. When the legislature, on the other hand, becomes dominant, the strong men there give their imprint to unfolding affairs.

Coalitions as tamers of powers

Continual shifts in leadership have enabled interest groups, despite built-in checks and balances, to form various coalitions to advance their specific causes. During the Roosevelt and the Truman regimes, for instance, organized labor had entry to the White House, while organized business turned to Congress. Again, on the issue of state versus Federal regulation, business has been in recent years for greater authority in the states; labor, for authority in the Federal government. Similarly, labor generally supports the Democratic party; and business, the Republican party. Without going into all the changes in coalitions over the years, the significant fact stands out that interest groups pick whatever governmental authority best suits their purposes in concrete situations and that these very choices tend by and large to checkmate one group against another. Thus, if organized labor was encouraged by the White House, Senator Taft and his team took up the cudgels for business at Capitol Hill.

The final result is not only a slowing down of the rate at which power is acquired by one group or another but also a better balancing and equalizing of power, which redounds to the stability and welfare of the entire community. For a while, labor may be in the ascendancy; for another while, business. But neither group can stay in the ascendancy too long.

The evidence almost justifies the identification of an unwritten federal system operating within the formal structure of our basic political federalism. If political parties have arisen outside the Constitution as centers of bargaining and compromise, so also has a complex multiplicity of associations, primarily of economic interests, arisen without any formal provisions in the Constitution. Though both political parties and interest groups attempt to exploit in various ways the complex authority of government for their ends, these groups, being free and equal–and aggressive–serve to checkmate each other. Indeed, they utilize the very checks and balances of our political agencies–executive, legislative, judicial, and, now, administrative as well–to reduce the danger of political absolutism. These multifarious checks may at times slow down, if not paralyze, the capacity of the government to act expeditiously enough to meet emergencies. The negative effect of our system of checks and balances, no doubt, looms as an urgent problem facing many democratic nations besides our own. Indeed, the tendency to immobilize government power reveals another facet of our basic moral dilemma. For the very nature of modern science and industry makes inevitable an enlarged orbit of political activity both at home and abroad. We, therefore, are faced with both the necessity of a large role for government and the perils of encroaching statism. How to preserve, at the same time, the checks and balances that tame political power and the adequate exercise of such power emerge as a central issue in the encompassing moral dilemma facing the second half of the twentieth century.

Fortunately, so far in our history, what had to be done in the interest of the national welfare was somehow done–even though a painful period of pulling and hauling preceded the specific action. Jefferson, for instance, effected the Lousiana Purchase prior to securing Congressional assent. Wilson led us, after some hesitation, on the side of the Western allies into World War I, as Roosevelt did into World War II. If an expansion of power is ever again needed, we may assume that, on the basis of the record thus far established, the responsible executive will be able to effect it and to keep within reasonable bounds or face the possibility of repudiation.

Does science need taming?

Even though science also has become large-scale, we do not face the same necessity of taming its power as we do that of business and government. For, the more active its growth, the better for mankind. We have become so fearful of the demonic aspects of nuclear discoveries that we forget that it is the application of the discoveries of science which has made possible our productivity, our standard of living, and our achievements in strengthening the economies of our Western allies and in advancing human welfare generally. The same science which we now fear is furnishing the means to free us from poverty, plagues, and enslavement. If we were to place a moratorium on science, we would thereby be imperiling progress, if not putting ourselves on the road to retrogression. What is more, the locus of contemporary danger growing out of scientific activity, as previously indicated, is not in science itself but in business and in politics; for the danger in science is, not in its power, but in the uses to which that power is put.

To be sure, scientists are perturbed by the danger to individual creativeness stemming from large-scale organization and, even more, by the long shadow of government subsidy and control. Their spokesmen accordingly give voice to various fears. Will the trend narrow the opportunities of the creative investigator eager to follow without fanfare or direction some hunch or interest of his own in pure research? Will those who supply the resources ultimately set all research goals and generally call the tune? Will the pressures for secrecy undermine the scientist's independence, threaten academic freedom, and put an end to the traditional internationalism of scientific findings? What of the temptation of political demagogues to conduct capricious and sensational investigations and thus threaten the independence so essential for scientists? It is under such pressures as these that scientists have joined the ranks of those who would tame government. Fortunately, their very spirit of dedication to truth places them firmly on the side of those who would be vigilant of liberty and democracy.

Morality and human association

Morality and ethics are in a unique way the outgrowth of human association. Constitutionalism, to be sure, is also the creation of human society, as are science, business, politics, government, and all the other major institutions which serve us and which we, in turn, serve. These come into existence, however, when man and his society have already achieved an advanced degree of cultural development; they are, in the main, the result of deliberate and purposive planning. The moral sentiments, on the other hand, are more spontaneous, come earlier, and grow out of the necessity of man to relate himself to the here and now and to the hereafter—to man, to his community, and to his God. These sentiments are formulated into precepts and codes by prophet and priest; eventually they become embodied in sacred scriptures—written and unwritten—to serve successive generations as a hallowed guide to life and action. Accompanying the sacred scriptures is a secular literature growing out of the wisdom of the ages in the never ending search for the moral life. And, whereas each individual may learn about constitutions, laws, science, and business through formal education as well as experience in adolescence and

adulthood, he acquires early in life his response to moral sentiments from his family, his church, and the spontaneous, natural
associations of his everyday environment.

Do moral values, then, serve to tame power? Many thought-
ful people are skeptical, if not actually discouraged, on this
score. They feel that the influence of these more intangible
values has failed to keep pace with large-scale material developments in business, government, and science. To be sure,
the primary institutions of family and church continue to condition with moral values the individual in the exercise of
power. But does the church in this secular age exert the influence it once did? Does the home shape character to the extent
that it did in a simpler period, when it was the center of life?
Who can deny that the abundance of material wealth frequently corrupts character—and sharpens the appetite for
power, whether it be the power of wealth, of position, or of
both? On the other side stands the reawakening of interest in
the enduring moral and cultural values of mankind. Universities and technical schools are revising curricula and exposing
students to the humanities and religion—to courses above and
beyond those yielding technical effectiveness in applying skills
—courses deemed indispensable for the responsible discharge
of power inherent in those skills.

Indeed, in spite of a probably less pervasive role played
by church and family, the very preoccupation of our generation
with moral issues may reflect a growing, rather than a diminishing, concern with social and ethical responsibilities. For
man, more on his own than he ever was, finds that freedom from
authoritative guidance may increase rather than diminish his
anxieties and perplexities. No matter how much he tries, he
cannot escape the ceaseless tension springing from his conscience for the consequences of his use of power, whether in

business, government, or any other area of responsibility. And so we come back to conscience as probably the most effective internal agency in man for taming power. There is, to be sure, the danger that conscience can be used to support self-delusion in the quest for power and glory by the unscrupulous and psychopathic. Power must therefore be constantly checked by counterpower, or by constitutionalism, or by both! But, as has been said so often, one cannot legislate or impose honesty, or integrity, or brotherhood. It is conscience, therefore, the intangible moral power carried within him by every man, that gives external, physical counterpower the sanction and the impetus that makes possible compromise, resolution, and compliance.

Tradition as tamer of power

Interwoven with morality are two additional outgrowths of human association which serve to tame power by emphasizing humane aspects. One is tradition. Each one of us is born into a social heritage, which, in addition to religious and moral sentiments, is made up of attitudes, codes of behavior, and values that shape our conduct in choosing between good and evil, between beauty and ugliness, between altruism and selfishness, between generosity and greed, and so on, through all the virtues we all aspire to acquire and to live by, whether we are deciding to establish a foundation to support worthy causes, to build a hospital, to overcome discrimination by hiring workers of a minority race, to endorse a center for the creative arts, or to put our shoulders behind a grass-roots reform movement in our home town.

It is this tradition which gives us confidence that we may be spared from the perversions of human liberty taking place under dictatorships. For this tradition makes up the heart of democracy—freedom, dignity of man, justice. This tradition is a power beyond formal law and government, giving us in whatever role we may be cast momentum to follow the best practice, to do the "decent thing," to eschew the mean and the ignoble, to be sensitive to the feelings of our neighbors in our relationships, and to respect the opinion of mankind in dealing with other nations. It is indeed a tradition followed alike by the agnostic and the atheist, by the religious and the devout.

Aesthetics as tamer of power

Finally, we must not overlook the potent force of man's imagination in creating out of his association with other men and nature the manifold expressions of beauty. Poetry, drama, painting, sculpture, music, architecture, all these expressions of the spirit and the aspirations of mankind make us pause in humility before the wonder of man and his works. It makes each of us kin with all men regardless of race or nation. For art is a universal language. No man can read Aeschylus, or Euripides, or Sophocles, or Shakespeare, or Goethe, or Tolstoi, or listen to the music of Verdi, or Beethoven, or Mozart, or Tchaikovsky, or look at the great paintings of the Renaissance in Italy, or Spain, or Holland, or Britain, or France, without being stirred and uplifted in mind and spirit. Indeed, in a world as divided as the contemporary one, it is heartening that art—particularly, painting, architecture, and music—is so free to cross national boundaries and to continue to enrich the common heritage of mankind.

We must not overlook the fact that even the artist is not without the failings of man, nor that all of us human beings are imperfect and in constant temptation of sin. The tyrant often serves as a generous patron of the arts. It is safer, consequently, when considering the dangers of power, to be on the whole pessimistic. History cautions against throwing off all available restraints against the abuse of power. That would be utopian, unrealistic, and dangerous. Nevertheless, we must not go to the other extreme of completely underrating man's intelligence and feeling for morality, decency, and beauty. For man and his society have created potent forces for shaping human conduct. Without these forces, counterpower as physical power would prove sterile—an armed neutrality, maintained only by the fear of mutual destruction—perhaps a necessity, but deadly in its effect on the human spirit. Fear alone can only serve to deter, not to inspire, or to create.

part three

THE CREATIVE USE OF POWER

10. *Negotiation: the stabilization and direction of power*

The taming of power represents an end result. It is to this that all our thinking has been directed. Yet taming alone is not enough; for, since power is essential for productivity and social progress, what we must really search for is not a taming that merely neutralizes and checks but, rather, one that canalizes and directs power from negative and destructive to positive and creative purposes.

If reason and human association tend to tame and direct power, we still need to ask: through what *activity* is this objective realized? If reason is a primary factor in marshaling power, how does it also bring forth constitutionalism with its ordered procedures for regulating this same power? How do men in separate associations arrive at accommodations and agreements which not only resolve differences from day to day but also crystallize precedents and modes of response as a

substitute for raw power in handling conflict? In the everyday
matter of industrial adjustments, how do changes in technology
become absorbed into established routines of work? How is the
expanding output of that work distributed? How do rules and
relationships linking men in their varying roles as workers,
consumers, and citizens—in mutual ties as well as continuing
differences—receive concrete formulation?

Negotiation the strategic activity

It is the negotiating process which constitutes the characteristic activity putting into play the varying procedures for taming and directing power. At first glance, negotiation may well
appear to be a weak and inadequate means for such an important task. Nevertheless it does embody the decision-making procedures within the daily contemporary scene—the patterns of
communications, the exchanges, the conferences, the demanding and counterdemanding, offering and counteroffering, the
threats to withdraw jobs or labor or goods from the market—all
these are strategic phases leading eventually to some kind of
settlement short of the use of raw power. Basic to all negotiations are three components: the amount of power that the negotiators bring to the conference, the type of power that they use,
and the kind of settlement each prefers to make rather than face
a showdown in which both take a risk of suffering loss. In business, negotiations are constantly going on in continuous transactions. Men with products to sell appraise the respective
powers of the men who want to buy; they sound them out in a
concurrent series of offers until a deal is consummated or the
transaction falls through. Where relationships are temporary,
as in the case of buyers and sellers, failure to agree may entail
nothing more than the withholding or transferring by each

party of its product to available competitive bidders. But, in negotiations within a framework of continuing relationships, whether in corporate policy making or in union-management bargaining, failure to agree may lead to threats, or actual tests of strength, such as resignations, strikes, or lockouts.

Constitutionalism—the product of negotiation

In politics, too, negotiation constitutes the characteristic, core activity. The very mechanism of the party system—the drafting of platforms, the nominations of candidates, the appeals to the electorate—is one continuous course of trying to meet and reach compromises satisfactory to the various interested factions which make up the strategic interest groups of the party. Similarly, after elections, the procedures of enacting and administering law, the pressures exerted on lawmakers and enforcement agencies by constituents back home and at the Capitol, the progressive compromises and conferences by which legislators hammer out conflicting demands, all these comprise a clear-cut chain of continuing negotiatory activities —as indeed does the succession of new statutes, with their executive acceptance or veto, their judicial interpretations, and possible further pressures for revision or replacement.

Our federal framework the result of negotiation

The decisions, compromises, and resolutions of issues by which the federal framework of our nation was constructed in 1791 represent the results of negotiation at its best. Within that framework, the age-old problem of central versus local authority has been continuously resolved in such a way as to provide constant adjustment to new needs. With the exception of the one recourse to raw power in the Civil War, the negotiating process has served to resolve profound differences between individuals and groups, custom and law, common law and statutory law, statutory law and the Constitution, and among the executive, legislative, and judicial branches of the government. While feeling has run high from time to time, and while drastic methods have been proposed now and then to modify the power of the judiciary or of the President, nevertheless we have managed to find a viable solution within the framework of the Constitution.

Diplomacy and negotiation

Diplomacy, of course, is the classical form of negotiation for adjusting the varying interests of nations. Power, as a counter in the scales of decisions, exerts an influence far more manifest and overt in international than in domestic affairs. For, in relations between nations, no system of law has yet been crystallized out of past negotiations to provide a framework of "due process" or rules of reason in settling conflicts of interest. Yet, recourse to naked power carries these days such a cataclysmic potential that, as Mr. Dulles and Mr. Adenauer as well as Mr. Bulganin and Mr. Khrushchev have pointed out, the very threat of the total destruction of the world as we know it may finally compel a negotiated settlement of peaceful coexistence between East and West. If America at present seeks answers to the impasse with Russia through coalitions, regional pacts, or balance of power on a world dimension, the hope yet remains primary that the achievement of a power equilibrium will persuade the Communist oligarchy in the Kremlin that, unless they wish to bring the world to the abyss of self-destruction, they must negotiate some orderly procedure for resolving differences and thus lay the foundation for coexistence among the nations of the world in spite of ideological differences.

Negotiation as an integrating activity

But negotiation as a way of adjusting differences among nations and thus avoiding warfare is only the most dramatic example of its central importance. Within the national scene, negotiation supplies nothing less than an integrating activity which makes it possible for our segmented and divided economy to operate as a whole. That our abundance is due to a division of labor and a specialization of function has by this time become axiomatic. This fragmentation, however, in assigning each one of us to his separate task and, at the same time, linking these tasks together in individual shops, enterprises, industries, and services, could not be carried forward without an effective method of administration—a method that recognizes the need for integration as well as specialization and for appropriate participation on the part of all those involved. To achieve such an objective, only two basic methods are available: one, the *authoritarian* method, historically the older, under which the prerogatives of making binding decisions are held by leaders with absolute authority; the other, the *negotiatory* method, under which the policies are evolved through discussion, conferences, even threats of withholding labor or property by strikes or lockouts—all of which lead ultimately to compromises and the best that can be obtained without resorting to a showdown of power.

Power a necessary ingredient in negotiation

It may well be that the rough exchange, the give-and-take, of negotiation too often yields untidy, inexact, and uncertain answers; but these imperfections are the price we pay for the freedom of bargaining and the equality of all parties at the conference table. Yet, behind the seeming untidiness, negotiation requires skills. Demands and counterdemands must be prepared with some idea as to their realism and practicability. Relevant information must be assembled. The scaling down of unreasonable demands must be persuasively presented in recognition of the rights of all parties. Finally, strategy and tactics must be developed to deploy power toward reaching desired goals by way of settlements that will facilitate accommodation among the negotiators.

Indeed, negotiation as a form of administration deserves intensive study, especially in this period when complex, large-scale institutional relationships have replaced the simpler, man-to-man dealings of an historically earlier stage. It is the only alternative to war between nations and to the disruption of productivity and cooperation within nations. It is the pervasive activity that not only tames but also employs power creatively toward the maximum degree of peace and accommodation that can be attained amid all the factors underlying a relationship. Power, indeed, with its capacity to punish or deprive, constitutes the indispensable prerequisite for negotiations. Without power on both sides no real negotiation takes place. The strong dominate; the weak retreat, submit, or play for time. Thus, prior to the organization of the auto workers by the United Automobile Workers—prior, that is, to the massing of the power of labor and the demonstrations of that power through strikes, sitdowns, picketing—no effective negotiations took place between the automobile companies and their employees. Similarly, the Russian Soviet leaders virtually refused to negotiate with the West until sufficient power had been built up through alliances, air bases, and materiel at strategic points in Europe to threaten the heartland of the Russian empire.

The negotiators thus take the measure of their own powers and of those with whom they negotiate as the leverage by which given ends may be promoted. The power equation must always be weighed. But this is not to say that power alone determines the outcome of any given negotiation. Since the negotiators remain men, they utilize other human endowments in their attempt to avoid the use of raw power. Reason enters into their calculations, and discussions of what can realistically be achieved with and without resort to power. Reason also recognizes time-honored precedents, as well as ever evolving new rules and decisions. Morality, tradition, imagination, also leave their imprint upon the negotiating activities. Thus, viable patterns of relationships are sought out within the power equation, with the hope of eventually relegating raw power into the background, even when sitting around the negotiating table. Moral sentiments enter into negotiations because the parties feel a need for justifying their successive positions by appealing to the decent opinion of mankind.

Use of power in negotiations to avoid resort to raw power

Since power constitutes a key factor in the very decisions that determine its uses, modern man must choose how best to arrive at such decisions. At one extreme is the situation of a single absolute wielder of power and the constant danger of resorting to violence as a way of maintaining dominance—the situation illustrated by Hitler, Stalin, and Mussolini. At the other extreme is that in which all parties attempt to wield power, with the danger of anarchy and again the use of vio-

lence one against the other. The third alternative is the middle
ground, in which the affected groups are impelled to establish
a balance of power under which they seek to reach compromises rather than resort to violence. Here again we see an illustration of the old truism, that as soon as we recognize the
essential and omnipresent role of power in human affairs, it
is not power as such but rather the manner of its use that becomes the crucial concern. Democratic Western nations seek,
above all, to avert violence in their exercise of power, not only
the destructive explosions of raw power into war, but also the
physical duress of police power compelling men to act against
their own conviction of right.

Of course, the dangers inherent in the recourse to sheer force
vary with the nature of the issues confronting the parties. In
the market place, for instance, potential buyers may refuse to
consummate a sale until the price comes within their range;
deliberate boycott, on the other hand, injects new issues concerning the use of power. So, too, the buyer who refuses to buy
until the asking price is satisfactory to him is in a different
power position from the one who lacks sufficient funds to buy
at all or at a price so low as to make it impossible to sell at a
reasonable profit.

But such transactions of traditional market theory hardly
reach the heart of the problem. More to the point are the efforts
in collective bargaining to avert the breakdowns that eventuate
in strikes, in the even more difficult endeavors to maintain the
diplomatic exchanges to avert the outbreak of war, and in the
establishment of procedures of due process to minimize revolts.
In these ever continuing, crucial relationships within which
we work and live, negotiators seek so to canalize power that
the area for resolving conflicts is widened by constructive de-

cisions and there is no longer the necessity of resorting to violence.

Test of strength for legitimate purposes reserved

The strategic words in this objective of narrowing and restricting recourse to raw power are the verbs *narrow, restrict, limit.* While each of these verbs suggests degree, each carries also the implication that freedom to resort to tests of strength–short of violence–under certain conditions never is completely abolished in a free society. For complete abolition of such recourse could be achieved only by surrendering to some supreme power all right of ultimate determinations in situations of difference. To be sure, not all recourses to tests of strength are permitted. Thus, violations of the collective rules of the shop by slowdowns and walkouts are forbidden; it is only upon the expiration of an existing agreement and prior to negotiating a new one that resort to strikes and lockouts is legitimate. When the legitimate spokesmen for the parties come to feel they cannot arrive at an agreement, the right to resort to the final test of economic strength remains an integral element of freedom and equality. None of them must sign on the dotted line unless or until he has appraised the costs of a trial by strength as too great or the results too uncertain to merit the gamble. Nor is this all. Men may deem the moral principles at stake so important that even defeat in an uncertain contest is preferable to piecemeal surrender by appeasement. What remains important is the right to choose alternative courses even after every effort has been made to reach agreement by negotiation.

Limitations on violence in use of power

Even in cases of disagreement in negotiating a contract, the effort to limit violence in the power tug is revealed in the progressive endeavors to regulate the nature, as well as the instruments, of outright conflict. In the event of a strike, for instance, union leaders and management officials negotiate the timing of a shutdown so as to safeguard machinery and equipment from damages. The violence that characterized strikes of the past was part and parcel of the organizational stage, when unions attempted to force—and employers resisted—the recognition of unions as the spokesmen for employees. Violence was the order of the day.

Likewise, in warfare, international rules and safeguards have been accepted for the treatment of prisoners and wounded and against the use of chemical and bacteriological weapons. However, in time of war, no one can feel confident that the rules of war will mitigate the cruelties of modern weapons, or that the rules of war will be observed at all. But, at least, the efforts to limit extreme violence continue unremittingly. It, indeed, is the professed aim of all nations to limit the use of nuclear weapons. Nor should it be forgotten that, as cruel and brutal as was World War II, not even Hitler dared to resort to chemical or bacteriological warfare. Perhaps fear of retaliation was a dominant motive, but that does not fully explain the matter. Fear is always a factor, the primary one. Yet, fear in itself did not prevent the bombing of cities or the invasion of neutral countries, though retaliation in such cases could be clearly foreseen.

To return to the domestic scene, it remains a prime premise of our democratic philosophy that no single individual or institution shall possess the power to enforce upon others decisions as to what to think, or what to know, or what to do. Correlatively, in the negotiation processes, all men and all associations possess equal opportunity to express themselves in the election of representatives, in the delegation of authority, in the procedures for conference, consultation, and settlement. To be sure, the realities of power do not always fulfill the specifications of such an ideal. As we scan the network of group associations, we cannot miss the differences in dimension, in membership, in strategic power. Business, for instance, while keeping within legal requirements for equal opportunity to others in appropriate circumstances, nevertheless wields great power by making available or withholding certain goods and jobs, by moving plants out of given localities and establishing them in others, by vesting leadership of high prestige in corporate officials. Also, by controlling the media of mass communications, newspapers, radio, and television, business exerts great influence in shaping attitudes and tests, in encouraging tendencies of a materialistic nature, and in discouraging others of an aesthetic nature. In politics, however, business corporations no longer have the vast influence to sway elections as they once had. Instead, they face increasingly the handicap of easily evoked suspicions against "the rich" and "the monopolists," traditionally a target for hostility throughout our history. Labor unions, in their turn, while acting as "his majesty's opposition" in the daily operation of a particular enterprise, nevertheless exert great economic power on the industrial front. Actually, a single international union, especially when organized on an industrywide basis, can shut down a whole basic industry if it suits its strategy. In industrial centers, unions also exercise great influence on the political front. Agricultural interests, too, while mustering an ever declining ratio of population, exert political strength beyond their numbers because of regional concentration and the traditional prestige of the farmer. And so we find tremendous diversities in the interests of the various associations and in the power of their

numbers, funds, prestige, and strategic positions in the social
and economic structure.

Coalitions as equalizers of power

How, then, among such diversities of power, are differences
resolved and agreements negotiated? The answer lies in coalitions—temporary or long-term—by means of which individuals,
associations, and nations of unequal power unite to promote
balances of power. The equality of strength brought about by
these alliances prevents the establishment of any single dominant, overriding power for any length of time. The same checkmating of strength makes negotiated decisions the practical
alternative to fighting it out. The most familiar example of
these shifting alliances and coalitions is found in the two-party
system, with each party representing groups of diverse sec-
tional, ethnic, and economic interests that negotiate their respective desires and programs in the compromises which go to
make up party platforms, nominations, and all the other activities that keep a party in power.

The coalition process by no means assures either an invariably fair alignment or a primary concern for moral values.
Soil and seaminess not infrequently accompany power. Deals,
logrolling, collusion, these are all considered the rewards of
alliances. Even presidents are nominated in smoke-filled rooms
by party politicians before the bursts of florid oratory make the
rafters ring in convention halls. Yet all this seamy side of
power is nothing but realistic observation, rather than a cause
for pessimism. For self-interest is a natural biological and
political fact, a characteristic of man in his eternal aspirations
and quest for power and glory. Since men differ in economic
and social positions, coalitions usually result in counterpower

as well as power. The deals that promote power alliances are incidents in the logic of power itself. Without some means of equalization, power is in danger of destroying the very freedom to negotiate which assures a voice in the decisions affecting liberty and welfare.

Moreover, it is the contrasts between alliances in democratic and in authoritarian societies that reveal the strategic differences. In a democracy, men in authority seek to use power through negotiation, without recourse to violence. In a totalitarian society, in contrast, power is wrested by leaders and imposed at will through violence, actual or threatened. In a democracy, only constitutional government may exercise coercive, physical power, and, even then, only within the safeguard of due process of law. Since, at any given moment, inequalities exist in the network of free and equal associations, we accept the fact that the need for law and orderly procedures can not be completely eliminated. The ability of government to deter and to punish must remain an essential of communal life, if only to restrain those who violate laws and regulations formulated within the constitutional system. In a democracy, again, the agencies that do apply coercion—the police and the military —are rigorously separated from those that formulate the policies they enforce. So deeply rooted are the traditions that make these agencies nonpolitical that the slightest indication that the frontiers may be crossed evokes the strongest kind of protest.

Principle of visibility as check on power

When dictators on the other hand seek to gain control, their strategic target becomes the capture of the police, the military, and, as a modern touch, they add the propaganda services! When the reins of power have been seized, moreover, the instruments of force no longer function as neutral services. They become the very agents for the suppression of any opposition as well as of any civil rights. And this fact yields us a third fundamental difference between democracy and authoritarianism. We might call it the *principle of visibility:* in a democracy, the maneuvers and the activities of alliances and coalitions are exposed sooner or later to the view of both the opposition and the public. It is impossible, for example, to envisage in America or in Britain such a secret and blurred dissolution of one alliance and establishment of another as resulted in Russia, first, in the removal and liquidation of Beria and, then, the demotion of Malenkov from the inner councils of power. Such an event in this country would have been reported in sensational headlines and over dramatic newscasts. Investigations would have been instituted—the party in office justifying its action, the opposition trying to prove wrongdoing, and each seeking the majority support in forthcoming elections. In Russia, the matter of Beria was coldly reported in a controlled press; people probably gasped but held their tongues; and soon a curtain of silence fell. Thus does the principle of visibility constitute in democratic nations a wide-reaching safeguard against the over-reaching of power drives by special interests, by parties, or by anyone already in office.

Alliances, in this country, continuously shift, thus providing one more method for adjusting the structure of power. For another thing, leaders are held responsible when policies do not work out, and they are replaced by electoral repudiation, by demotion, or by whatever disciplinary action may be imposed under law. Alliances may even be dissolved and new realignments formed. In authoritarian countries, only through war, or revolution, or assassination, or liquidation, may leaders be removed or coalitions changed. To repeat, in the alliances behind

democratic negotiation, there is always the possibility of changing sides and of balancing the power groups—without running
any risk to life or liberty.

Reason and morality in negotiations

What about the importance of reason and morality in negotiations? Since reason and morality serve as tamers of power,
as we have seen, one might ask to what extent are they actually
used in the negotiation process. The answer is that they are
continually used. The principle of visibility and the consequent
need for convincing all parties, including the uncommitted
public, lead each party to a constant effort to justify its own
position logically and morally. When parties confront one another—be it in conventions, legislative hearings, union-management sessions, stockholders meetings—their overt power and
their interests constitute the *implicit* counters of the negotiating process. But, in their efforts to support their demands and
to combat those of the other side, each side appeals to logic—
rational criteria and arguments—and each invokes ethics—moral
values such as justice, equity, and the general welfare. Thus,
reason and morality actually constitute the *explicit* counters of
the negotiating process.

It would be naive to suggest that the parties in negotiation
thereby seek justice above all, and will make sacrifices merely
for the sake of logic and morality. A realistic study of history
dispels any such view. On the other hand, the opposite attitude,
that the invoking of logic and ethics is only so much "double
talk," is equally unjustified. For one thing, in most of the matters that come up for negotiation, the facts and the equities are
not always clear-cut for one side or the other. Indeed, the issues, as to how to resolve conflicts about facts and equities, are

usually embedded in all sorts of ambiguities, in which the interests and the convictions are clear enough but the facts and the principles are in dispute. Even among specialists, wide differences of opinion exist at any given time regarding the best alternative among available courses. What criteria, for example, should be applied in setting wages at a given juncture so as to best meet the aspirations of wage earners for improved living standards, the pressures of costs and competition upon management, and the stake of the whole community in productivity, lower prices, and stable money value? What method of taxation at a given period will assure equities among income classes, yield incentives for investors and enterprisers, and, at the same time, safeguard the national interest in adequate revenue and a sound fiscal policy? Questions such as these have no clear-cut answer, yet hardly an area of negotiation but raises parallel uncertainties of fact and values.

In the absence of absolute authority, who shall define amid these uncertainties the line of reasoning, the technical criteria, and the ethical values that shall determine the decision to be made? It becomes inevitable that an appeal must be made to rational criteria and to moral values, these in turn to be assimilated into the tactics of negotiation. It is not surprising, therefore, that one is seldom sure whether a protagonist is sincere in thus invoking logic and morality or is using them primarily as a respectable gloss on his power position. Indeed, in the exchanges with which the negotiators attempt to establish their respective cases, there not infrequently appears a species of rationalization—where economics proves whatever the parties want proved, and morality sanctions whatever they demand.

Such manipulation, or rationalization, is familiar to our psychologically sophisticated age; the processes have been widely explored in studies of individual psychopathology.

Rationalization there expresses itself in intellectual and ethical distortions, by which one finds justifications for socially unacceptable, unconscious desires. Motives that violate the conscience and the code of right behavior thus need the disguises of rationalization or moralization.

The rationalizing and the moralizing that appear in negotiations, on the other hand, represent quite another category of behavior. Reasons and justifications advanced at the conference table are not as a rule intellectual or ethical distortions disguising hidden motivations. As a matter of fact, the negotiators know quite well what they want to take away from the sessions. The arguments and justifications they mobilize therefore are, in part, convictions and, in part, weapons in the strategy and tactics of bargaining. In wage negotiations which may affect prices and availability of goods to consumers, for example, the parties would like to obtain not only the consent of their immediate constituents but also the understanding and the goodwill of the entire community. But one of the parties may seek also to outsmart the other to make a good deal for its side. Accordingly, one finds the appeals to economic criteria and moral values—as, for example, costs of living, rising standards of living, a share in "the more abundant life," purchasing power, capacity to pay, productivity, and competitive conditions, all of which are so frequently invoked in wage negotiations—are not unconscious rationalization but conscious tactical use of data and precepts selected to lend a logical and moral atmosphere to the goals sought.

In other words, the negotiators put forth what might be called *social equations* to justify the drives of group interests and the claims for specific demands as being good for the nation and being sanctioned by democratic values. These social equations are quite different from unconscious rationalizations stemming from the aggressions of neurotic personalities. They are deliberately used as a tactic in their strategy.

Under a constitutional framework, however, there is a limit to which men of power may exploit the beliefs and values of the people they lead. Indeed, in this respect, the differences between negotiatory and authoritarian societies are crucial. The extremes of distortion—distortion perpetrated by dictators in compelling obedience to policy, and in identifying policy, however shifting, with truth and righteousness—have become familiar portents of the potential for evil in our age of science and technology. For the instruments of communication—radio, television, press, cinema—have attained a reach and an impact over men's minds never before even imagined. Nor are we in our democracy completely free from such dangers. On the contrary, in our newspapers, over our broadcasts, and on our screens, we experience recurrently the reckless manipulations of demagogues and their power tactics—scapegoating, fear mongering, and high-pressuring. But precisely because these manipulations take place in a continuing atmosphere of negotiation, before long, the demagogue runs his course. Opponents talk back. The most vociferous demagogue sooner or later finds his versions of truth and morality challenged and exposed. Fortunately, in the free market place of ideas, all versions have to stand up against the enduring values and standards of decency and justice embedded in our national traditions.

Built-in principle of gradualism in negotiatory society

Indeed, our traditions, stemming as they do from Anglo-Saxon constitutionalism, yield still another restraint upon power, that of *gradualism*. In spite of the seeming noisiness and the sporadic local violence, we seek on the whole adaptations through orderly patterns of change and advance. The very dynamics of science and technology, creating as they do ceaseless pressure toward new methods and, by that token, new ways of life, create an inevitable and interdependent requirement for political and social adjustment. In a negotiatory society like ours, with some interest groups demanding and others opposing reforms, with both sides constantly debating the pros and cons and frequently checkmating each other, even the most urgent of adjustments may lag. It is encouraging to note, however, as we review our history, that the discussions and debates surrounding major issues—universal education, women suffrage, social legislation, collective bargaining, equality of opportunity, minority rights—result, true after much hauling and pulling and at times local intransigence, in an orderly acceptance of reforms. Only in such a way could American society deal with the problems of technical growth and advancing ethical responsibilities.

In authoritarian societies, in contrast, established channels for reform are denied affected groups. Maladjustments build up; resistance and revolt go underground. The police state then takes over. Spying and informing are encouraged. Concentration camps are instituted for the suspect. Purges are initiated as a way of striking terror into anyone tempted to lead a revolt. Cruelty mounts upon cruelty until the people become apathetic, losing whatever hope they may have ever had for attaining the freedom and the dignity of man.

Just to reflect upon such an alternative puts a fresh light on our own procedures. For the question may well be asked: do the processes of negotiation, even though they tame power, promote a moral society? The answer, to be sure, is clouded.

Beyond the measure of commitment felt by most negotiators to the values of American democracy—dedication to freedom, human dignity, and progressive improvement—a species of manipulation may, as we have seen, enter into the trading at conference sessions and legislative halls. Yet, in spite of deals and at times even collusiveness, how best may we arrive at moral ends in a democracy? By explicitly formulated once-and-for-all goals? It is fortunate, in a deeper sense, that such goals do not appear on the agenda of legislative proceedings, collective bargaining sessions, and all the other procedures of give-and-take. Only authoritarians and fanatics are certain of ultimate goals and of how to achieve them. What, after all, *is* a just price, an adequate wage, a desirable rate of production? Who can justify by sheer logic, or ethics, or aesthetics, a new commodity or service; or the spending of money on advertising to create a new demand whether it be for an unnecessary gadget, or an air conditioner, or a recorded classic? Simply to ask these questions indicates that discussion, conference, bargaining, negotiation, is the only free, nonauthoritative (perhaps the best) moral way of arriving at decisions now available to man.

Compromise and accommodation in a negotiating atmosphere among equals are not ways of appeasement but, rather, ways of resolving differences, which reckon with power but stop short of invoking it in its destructive forms. At the same time, there is no guarantee that negotiation by itself will always yield decisions that advance us on our way toward ethical goals; for, fundamentally, equity, security, and freedom must emerge, not from techniques of bargaining, but from the character of the men engaged in these negotiations and from the moral values of the society of which they are part. Negotiation constitutes nothing less than a prime form of communica-

tion among men performing the daily tasks of living and working in industrial democracy. It thus provides a way of dealing
with what has been recognized for some time as a major problem: how to establish effective communication in a society as
complex as ours. Negotiation entails an awareness that men
now group themselves into associations to promote common
objectives and must offer to other associations something they
can give in exchange for what they want. Since both sides
possess power, they respect each other. For, if they resort to a
showdown, both sides must pay some penalty and incur some
loss. It pays, therefore, to agree. With this assumption in mind,
each side is forced to probe for the limits within which agreement may be reached and to seek formulations which will
resolve conflicts into structures of accommodation.

Negotiation as a form of communication

Negotiation also facilitates communication in helping to integrate, as already indicated, the activites which make up our
specialized way of life. Thus, not only across institutional lines
but also within organizations themselves negotiation offers the
best medium of communication to attain maximum participation and consent, especially under the recent trend in business
toward decentralization. To the degree that managements seek
to promote communication among leaders, subordinates, and
the ranks in terms that recognize the essential dignity and
equality of all involved, to that degree does the structure of
power move toward cooperative alignment. Leaders and men
become aware that they share common interests. Assured that
their differences also will get a hearing, they find a truer security; and communication moves toward the give-and-take of
negotiation. Disciplines in daily work remain a requirement of

industrial operation, as does observance of red and green lights in traffic regulation. But, within the framework of negotiation, all these disciplines emerge as accepted work rules, mutually formulated, established, and endorsed, rather than as commands imposed from above.

Negotiation and unfinished business

Finally, negotiation may prove the soundest way of assuring freedom. For, with negotiation as the key to progressive human relationships, man's advance is conceived of as unfinished business. Thus a new light is thrown upon the survival value of capitalist democracy for human society and upon the skepticism expressed by many critics that capitalism can ever furnish the habitat of a progressive community. These critics assume that, with the abolition of private property, materialistically motivated business managers will be replaced by dedicated, selfless servants of the state. Events have by now clearly demonstrated that before very long the selfless servant, in fact, turns into an absolutist commissar. Such is the logic of power. The gradual gains growing out of the exchanges of negotiation in our capitalist democracy, on the other hand, furnish convincing evidence of steady advance toward social goals without the risk of enthroning commissars; for capitalism as it has evolved in the West is a decentralized form of power—in contradiction to Marxian theory—with negotiation as the strategic form of administration. If concern tends to be focused equally upon the production of goods through science, technology, and business and upon their distribution through political activities reinforced by moral sanction, we should expect to find this double concern reflected in the agenda of specific negotiations. And precisely this concern is what we do find in the procedures of collective bargaining, legislative halls, conventions, and all the other expressions of constitutionalism, which guide the power of nature and man toward agreed-upon standards of progressive improvements.

So important, indeed, is this activity of negotiation that only as we grasp its full import do the major issues confronting the nation become understandable. Thus, the struggle over liberty, traditionally an image of the power struggle, is in one sense part of the endless fight for freedom to negotiate to assure maximum opportunity not only in terms of self-fulfillment but also in terms of doing one's job to the best of one's ability. We have witnessed this battle in recent years: first, in the struggle of labor to have unions accepted as legitimate institutions to represent it in negotiations with industry; and, then, in the effort of business to conserve, through these same negotiations, freedoms deemed essential by management to keep its enterprises productive and profitable. Academic freedom, again, is a prerogative from which scholars cannot afford to retreat, for that is the only climate of negotiation in which they can safeguard their most cherished work conditions, pursuing truth themselves as well as training and encouraging their students to pursue the truth. Similarly, we all defend the Bill of Rights from being eroded in order to safeguard our capacity for carrying on as citizens the multiple and complex tasks of negotiation governing our democracy, from union office and local precinct to the legislative halls and executive mansions of state and nation. Freedom of association becomes a cherished right, because it in turn makes possible the mobilization of power in the negotiatory process for a more equitable distribution of the wealth of industry and for the leisure necessary not only for a rising standard of living but also for the cultivation of spiritual and aesthetic values.

And so, in this way, negotiation—with its give-and-take and at times even compromise, with its obeisance to economic, political, and moral values—turns out to be the democratic way of free men, facing always the unfinished business of realizing self-fulfillment in human society.

11. *America—fear or faith?*

As we come to the end of our exploration of power and morality in American society, we inevitably return to the question posed at the beginning of the book: Why are we Americans obsessed with fear and uncertainty? What are we afraid of anyhow! Do we need to be defensive?

The values of our tradition are democratically conceived, pragmatic, subject to continual testing and modification. We enjoy a built-in system of checks and balances, which prevents any one group from holding power for very long unless it has the consent of the community, as well as ethical justification. And yet we smart under the accusations made against us that we are a business civilization, primarily materialistic and profit-minded. Indeed, it would seem that we ourselves share these views and, in fact, suffer feelings of guilt because of them. For these reasons, Americans in all walks of life seem to react with defensiveness and overaggressiveness not only in their internal relationships at home but also in their external relationships abroad. Indeed, the fear that President Eisenhower admonished us against may be rooted in this very defensiveness. Otherwise, how explain at the peak of our power the obsessive fears shown in our dealings with one another and with other nations?

Surely we are not—whatever the degree of espionage and subversion—in such danger of being destroyed from within as heresy-hunters, official and unofficial, would have us believe. Nor do our allies mean to show lack of respect for our leadership, or lack of appreciation for our generosity, when they question our judgment of how best to contain as well as to negotiate with Russia or the so-called neutral nations.

Fear, confusion, and overaggressiveness

Underlying these symptoms of fear—defensiveness, confusion, overaggressiveness—is a lack of confidence in our own ethical values, an uncertainty concerning ways and means to resolve the ever present conflict between power and morality. These symptoms are born in the misunderstanding of oneself and the group to which one belongs—its values, its traditions, and the way it meets the aspirations inherent in the eternal virtues of decency, kindness, justice, and humanity.

How, then, are we to overcome fear and achieve sufficient insight into the ethical dilemma confronting us that we may live in peace with our own inner selves and carry on an acceptable partnership with one another at home and with our allies abroad? How can we achieve that confidence which commands respect at the negotiating table without conveying threats of power? How can we achieve the poise that breeds respect but not fear?

The first step in such a quest must be the frank recognition that power, instead of being a burden and evil, is an asset, a prerequisite for effective leadership. Without power one cannot assume responsibility, or advance progress, or, indeed, achieve freedom. For those who have power do not share it willingly with those who do not have it unless confronted with the possibility of punishment, or loss, or such radical modification of power that to give up some of it is the better part of discretion. Again, without power one cannot assure peace. A potential aggressor must always realize that, if he overreaches himself, he runs the risk of armed resistance and the possibility of ultimate defeat.

Business as a system of power

The next step is to face frankly—and without apologies—the fact that business, no less than government, is a system of power. Indeed, it must have power—largely economic in nature —if it is to mobilize the resources, the labor, the materials, and the capital to produce and distribute the goods necessary for a constantly rising standard of living, and to respond to the needs of government for an adequate defense establishment and such assistance to our allies as to keep them in a position of self-respect and strength.

But business cannot achieve these objectives unless, as part and parcel of employing power for the positive use of creating wealth and service, it also enjoys the power to deprive, to punish, and to discipline. Business must have the power to withhold jobs and income in exchange for the opportunity to work and share in the proceeds. It must be able to demand a price for its products and services which will yield a profit and provide enough surplus for replacements, research, and experiment. Thus power works both ways—to enrich and to deprive. Therein lies the moral dilemma inherent in the conduct of business enterprise.

Business and government convert findings of science into usable wealth

Though it is science which yields the secret of natural energy and so the basic power responsible for our wealth and material strength, it is business which converts the findings into usable goods and services for the consumer. Government also plays a similar role in making available such tax-supported services as mail and postal deliveries, roads, health, education, and social security. In war emergencies, it becomes directly or indirectly the major producer and consumer of all goods. Increasingly government even during times of peace is undertaking multipurpose economic enterprises which are too large and costly for private business, such as conservation, flood control, navigation, and public power. The Tennessee Valley Authority, the Bonneville Dam, and the St. Lawrence seaway are examples. Without business and government, the findings of science would be just so much new data advancing learning, intellectually interesting but little more.

Science too is a system of power. But, until its findings are converted into energy in the practical world to create wealth, the power of science is amoral, ethically neutral—a point which escapes those who frown upon science as destructive in its influence in the modern world. It is those who convert the power of nature into energy for practical use—the businessman and the politician, not the scientist—who face the ethical issues of good and evil.

The technical "must" versus the ethical "ought"

Unlike scientists, businessmen operate partly in a moral universe and partly in an amoral universe. On the one hand, businessmen may not, like scientists in their laboratories, disregard the moral implications of what they do. For the businessman is involved with people as employees, as fellow executives, as government representatives, as investors, as consumers, all of whom may not agree with him in his decisions, particularly as these decisions affect them in their respective individual and group roles. On the other hand, the businessman is a technician, administering impersonally a system of power through an institution that must remain efficient, solvent, and profitable. This is the businessman's amoral universe. Thus, a business executive in his daily job may be compelled to do things which inescapably confront him with grave moral conflicts. These conflicts are especially acute when his decisions adversely affect human welfare, as in laying off or discharging employees, reducing wages and dividends, increasing prices to consumers, or moving an enterprise to another community, or, even worse, shutting down a plant completely.

Here is the heart of the moral dilemma confronting the businessman. He is immersed, day in, day out, in issues raising the technical "must" against the ethical "ought." The conflict is sharpened for him by the fact that his own self-interest may be involved in the decision he makes. This morally ambiguous position makes it difficult for him to divorce himself enough from a given situation to be sure that his decision is technically the soundest and at the same time the most consistent with justice to all parties concerned. To add to his moral dilemma, he does not have the criteria—even with regard to technical soundness—to which a scientist may turn for testing, measurement, and approval by his peers. Profitability and productivity, the usual standards of managerial effectiveness, are themselves the result of judgment, in which self-interest, again, may play a large role. And, even in the absence of self-interest, personal judgment, lacking rigorous criteria for testing, is liable to considerable error. Thus any given decision is most likely to be biased in the interests of financial prudence, even though costly to human values. In any close decision, in other words, the responsible businessman is most likely to resolve the issues in favor not only of conserving the power entrusted to him but also of maintaining this power at high levels of efficiency for the creation of goods and services. By doing so, he reasons, not without logic or even moral justification, that he will render the greatest service to the community in the long run.

This conflict between what is technically sound and socially just is sharpened by the ingrained suspicion that all power is dangerous, evil, and corrupting—unless tamed and directed. And, certainly, historical experience seems to confirm this suspicion, whether in the realm of politics or business. During the nineteenth century, business was exploitative and, with notable exceptions, indifferent to the welfare of the community. And, in those days, if any businessman's conscience troubled him, he could always find comfort in contemporary economic and moral doctrines which put a premium on hard work, thrift, and the pursuit of self-interest.

Other power systems as checks on business

Business, however, is not the only power system operating in our democracy. Other power systems in our society, in fact, develop checks and counterpower to business. These counterpower systems are continuously at work—particularly those

political in nature. If we extend the realm of politics to trade
union, agrarian groups, consumer associations, as well as
corporate organizations, we end up with a pluralistic system of
power, the parts checking and counterchecking each other in
daily dealings as well as in the larger arena of legislative halls
and executive offices. Indeed, perhaps no other segment of the
economy has been under such sharp scrutiny during the past
quarter of a century as business. Government, labor, farmers,
and various consumer groups have been more than unfriendly
critics: they have been even hostile, and thus have given rise to
the perplexity in which businessmen find themselves in justifying their function in society.

Interdependence of power systems

For it must always be remembered that all systems of power
are interrelated and interdependent. Without mutual respect
and acceptance—even though the widest differences may prevail on concrete issues—it is impossible to operate a viable democracy. In a free society, reckless attacks must be held to a
minimum; exaggeration and distortion must be discounted as a
phase of political activity, to be forgotten the day after elections or negotiations or whatever the occasion when hard bargaining takes place. In other words, to survive and prosper, a
free society must achieve a balance of power and an inner co-
herence, just as on a global scale nations must achieve a balance of power and some agreement on moral values if peace is
to prevail.

However interdependent the various powers may be, some
control and direction must be provided. For this purpose, supreme sovereign power is placed in the hands of government.
But, even here, such power is defined and limited in the Constitution. It then becomes one of the primary functions of govern-

ment to strive for an equality of opportunity among individuals and groups. Otherwise, there would be no way of preventing those who happen to be the strongest at a given moment from exploiting the weaker and injuring the common welfare.

Moral system as check through conscience

In addition to checks and counterchecks as a way of taming power, the moral code through conscience acts as a prime control. Thus every wielder of power carries within himself a built-in check prodding him constantly with the question, "Am I exercising power with justice and mercy?" As we know, conscience and the moral code are implanted in us early in life, growing firmer and more effective as we pass from adolescence to maturity. Thus, conscience and the moral code influence and shape a man long before he takes on a job in the workaday world. We are already men of conscience before we become businessmen, politicians, or scientists. We are men of conscience before we become wielders of power. What moral tension exists in the power wielder therefore stems from this source. Other power groups may check him *politically*—but he too may counter power with power and resist pressure to do something he does not deem wise, provided he is willing to pay the price. In other words, he can use power as a countertactic. But no one can very well be tactical with his own conscience. Moreover, though conscience is not endowed with any physical power to punish or to deprive, and its thrusts are imponderable and intangible, yet, of all power systems, it has perhaps the most compelling influence over man. Indeed, he who offends his conscience too deeply and consistently may wind up in such serious inner conflict as to succumb to emotional or mental illness.

Conscience and counterpower both necessary

The constant moral tension to which an executive is subject is highly desirable; it serves as a pervasive check against arbitrariness, capriciousness, and injustice. But conscience alone may not be potent enough to withstand temptations toward self-aggrandizement. The pages of history are filled with the tragic consequences of the overweening ambition of kings, politicians, businessmen, the clergy, revolutionists, and counter-revolutionists. Such tyrants always find moral justification for what they feel they have to do. Conscience may make cowards, but it also makes self-deceivers, especially among those who lust for power. Counterpower therefore must be forever in the offing to restrain and to thwart those who would exact a gain without offering any reasonable quid pro quo. In extreme cases it even becomes necessary to inflict punishment for violations of reason, law, and morality. That is to say, both conscience and fear of loss or actual punishment must always work together as a deterrent to keep abuse to a minimum.

Negotiation as stabilizer and director of power

While power is a necessity, it must be tamed, stabilized, and directed not only for the obvious reason of averting resort to violence but also for advancing individual and group welfare. Rules of the game must be formulated so that conflicts of interests may be resolved without resort to naked power. Negotiation constitutes, as we have seen, the characteristic American activity for realizing this objective. It is in the political convention, in the union-management conference, in the committee hearing, in the caucus, and in the legislative chambers that the claims of various interest groups are heard and discussed, differences resolved, accommodations effected.

In a negotiatory atmosphere, reason, logic, emotions, and power are all invoked to bring about the best possible outcome for each party. But, once an agreement is reached, conflict over the major distribution of power is resolved. To avoid indefinite commitment to an agreement in which important issues have been compromised, the parties may, as in the case of union contracts, limit its duration to a fixed term, or, as in the case of constitutions, provide for methods of amendment. When it is then time to negotiate a new agreement or to draft a new constitution, logic, emotion, and power are employed once more in an effort to gain more favorable terms. Under each negotiation, rules are worked out for the handling of such differences as may arise even under the agreement. Power is stabilized, and rights are defined for each of the parties. Some have a right to initiate new measures; others, the right to challenge. In the event that differences arise, discussion under defined procedures takes place. If necessary, a judicial agency is invoked; and its decision settles the issues in conflict. In a dynamic democracy, it is a prima-facie fact that all conflicts and all differences can never be settled at one stroke. With ever changing conditions and shifts of power, conference and negotiation again must be a continuous process. The only alternative is to impose decisions through dictatorship.

Reason and logic thus play an important role in the process of stabilizing power. Reason supplements conscience as a guide to behavior. Reason helps to bring forth constitutionalism as an ordered procedure under which power is best exercised within rules agreed upon among individuals and groups affected. The systems of jurisprudence and codes of ethical practice which have developed as a result of negotiation in government, in

industry, and in professional associations are all applications
of logical thought to the stabilization and control of power.

The propensity toward human association also acts as a
stabilizer of power. As man interacts with others for various
purposes, that very interaction sets limits upon his complete
freedom of action. Mutual interests and needs must be taken
into consideration. And so it is that out of constant interaction
ethics develop, traditions cumulate, as guides for fair dealing
between competitors, colleagues, superiors, and subordinates.
Imagination becomes heightened as man works and plays with
other men. Literature, music, painting, sculpture, architecture,
take shape as forms of communication, create a common language, and widen horizons enabling man to transcend his greed
and lust for power. His egotism is sublimated by a higher
vision of humaneness and a sense of fitness in dealings with
other men.

And, so, man as a wielder of power is inevitably confronted
with the necessity of sheathing power before the equity and
dignity of those who associate with him. Although in any negotiation he may yield or compromise on this or that point, he is
assured thereby of living in greater comfort with himself and
his fellow men. Thus conscience, reason, morality, tradition,
and imagination together propel man and his community
toward a system of law as a safeguard against the abuse of
power, and toward the moral and aesthetic life as a way of ful-
filling his hopes and transcending the temptations of the flesh.

The American tradition: negotiation under constitutionalism

Negotiation is embedded in the very core of the American
tradition. Its logic and its necessity grew out of the forces pres-

ent at the birth of the nation—forces which have continued to play a dominant role throughout our history. We think of 1776 primarily as the year that witnessed the promulgation of the Declaration of Independence. But two other fateful forces, one a mechanical invention, the other a doctrine, were also projected upon the world at approximately that time: Watt's steam engine and Adam Smith's *Wealth of Nations*. The first embodied the technical application of the power of science to the production of goods. It was the beginning of a process leading ultimately to mechanization, mass production, and, most recently, to automation. It gave us the key to unlock an enormous potential in productivity and material wealth. The second, Smith's *Wealth of Nations*, implicitly sanctioned the use of economic power in the pursuit of self-interest in the accumulation of wealth. The Declaration of Independence, for its part, pledged the power of government toward the realization of life, liberty, and the pursuit of happiness. In a fundamental sense, the history of our nation is a history of the weaving of these three strands into a synthesis of material and moral power, or, to put it in the language of this book, a history of one continuous negotiation to reconcile and put into a working equilibrium the power of science and technology, the power of industry, the power of politics, and the power of the moral code—all in the interests of the common welfare.

Our forefathers clearly recognized the necessity of power as a strategic ingredient of action and progress. They also realized at the same time, however, that power unless tamed, stabilized, and directed would inevitably lead to victory of the strong and exploitation of the weak. Hence, power was defined and distributed among the Federal government and the states, as well as among the three branches of government, legislative, executive, and judicial. The negotiating activity was provided within the framework of our Constitution–the Constitution it-self was the result of ceaseless negotiating activity. Indeed, the legislative process, including that of amendment, became a matter of continuous negotiation. Later, similar systems of con-stitutionalism were gradually adopted by nongovernmental groups–farmers, workers, businessmen, professional societies –so that both within each group and across all the groups a system of check and countercheck prevails.

In actual life, however, one group or another may at times get the upper hand. But not for long. Sooner or later a balance of power becomes established, for all groups realize that only with such a balance can compromise and accommodation be achieved. Indeed, if any group or special interest steps out of bounds and overreaches itself, government steps in with the necessary legislation to establish equality of bargaining power. Thus it acts as an umpire to carry out what it had been pledged to do from the very beginning, namely, maintain a system under which all may enjoy equality of opportunity.

This system of negotiation is no doubt untidy; it leaves many problems unsolved. Nevertheless, within its framework a con-tinental nation has been able to resolve its differences ami-cably. With the single exception of the Civil War, resort to naked power has been avoided. The result has been a decentral-ized system of business–with tens of thousands of individual enterprises competing with one another for the favor of the community. By the middle of the twentieth century, a powerful labor movement had arisen, winning for its members a stand-ard of living unequaled elsewhere either now or in the past. Most recently, the freedoms embraced in the Bill of Rights and the Constitution received powerful support when the imprima-tur of the Supreme Court was placed upon the doctrine of

equality by forbidding the practice of segregating children in
public schools on the basis of color.

Social morality an evolving concept

At the same time, there is no authoritative moral guide imposed by government, church, or any other institution. Authoritative and binding decisions are made only through a constitutional process, gradually and slowly, within appropriate rules,
which are themselves negotiated by the parties. Out of this
moral climate of freedom has grown an indigenous philosophy
characteristically American—the philosophy of pragmatism. It
eschews doctrinairism; its claims are modest, a working kind
of philosophy constantly testing theories or opinions by results.
It abjures absolute truths. It boasts of no abstruse metaphysical
structure. Argument and counterargument are left, rather, to
examination and modification as people interact and negotiate
their divergent interests. Morality thus becomes a continuous
quest, to be socially and politically implemented as situations
change. And, while we accept the eternal verities as handed
down in sacred literature, we are not content to rest on mere
verbal homage. On the contrary, we continuously urge the application of these verities to the here and now so that the kingdom of God may be realized on earth as well as in heaven.

Moral tension intrinsic in business function

In such an atmosphere of continuous quest for the just and
moral life, business, like all other forms of organized activity,
remains under constant scrutiny and challenge. As an administrator of a production unit, a businessman may enjoy considerable power, and the business system as a whole enjoy great
power. Yet this power is checked on all sides by that of other

systems. Because businessmen now make their crucial decisions within the framework of due process, other groups are
free to challenge, review, modify, or veto. Businessmen, moreover, like the rest of us, are subject to the conditioning of the
moral code and are under constant moral tension in their
double-faceted jobs as amoral technicians and as human administrators.

What business now needs more than anything else therefore
is the conviction that its function is morally justified. None of
us can put forth his best effort if the moral value of what he
does is questioned by his fellow men. Indeed, who can carry
the burdens of life unless he enjoys the satisfaction that what
he does serves to advance human dignity and welfare? Part of
the defensiveness of businessmen undoubtedly derives from
the fact that they have been criticized and attacked without always having been confronted with a clear bill of indictment.
We would all be the gainers if we were more tolerant than we
are of the margin of error to which businessmen, like the rest
of us fallible human beings, are subject. We would strengthen
the hand of him who would serve. Without some such favorable
attitude on the part of the community, business in the long run
cannot do its most effective job in converting the findings of
science into a richer life and creating the strength necessary
to meet the obligations of world leadership in war and in peace.

Businessmen, of course, cannot expect such understanding
as a free gift; they must earn their trust by the manner in which
they exercise power. Moreover, they must be ready to accord
to the administrators of other power systems the same equality
of opportunity they themselves seek. They must learn not to
dictate but to negotiate with labor, farmers, consumers, and
government.

Perils to the American system

And, as a people, we must also learn to exercise our power as sovereign citizens with patience and justice, and in accordance with the spirit of due process. Since, in the interest of democracy, we wish to preserve our decentralized system of industry, we have no other recourse but to support its administrators even as we check them in the interests of a progressive, free society.

Unless we all—as Americans, whatever our place in society—exercise our powers with tolerance we are in danger of bringing our house down upon ourselves. For, to the extent that peril threatens, the peril is within, not without. To maintain a society like ours requires wisdom and patience—at times, indeed, self-sacrifice. Only as we look back in historical perspective can we see the working out of relative justice in given situations. The very science, for example, which yields the necessities, comforts, and strength in an ever larger measure, is also disruptive. While it enables business and government to create wealth for a higher standard of living, it also generates vast technological and economic change and consequent instability. Although science in the long run makes the growth of new industries and jobs possible, it also in the short run makes established industries obsolete, abolishing customary jobs and skills overnight. Business, in its turn, while in the long run enriching the community, by creating new industries, gives rise in the short run to irregularities, seasonal and cyclical, with resulting unemployment and displacement. Although over any generation the nation becomes wealthier and the standard of living higher, in the here and now those least able are frequently called upon to suffer the financial and social hardships

entailed by progress. We have, of course, increasingly provided, primarily through government, measures for tiding over
those who temporarily lose out—unemployment compensation,
pensions, and other welfare programs. Nevertheless, most of
these measures are at best stopgaps and palliatives. It is in a
sense ironic that so far in our history only the crises of defense
and war—and the production they induce—have afforded our
people the opportunity of full production and full employment.

This is not to say that we shall not develop more adequate
means of stabilizing the economy even as we encourage its
growth to ever greater productivity. But, until the required
procedures are tested and perfected, it is too much to expect the
rank and file of citizens to suffer willingly the hardships of
economic fluctuations inherent in free enterprise, even though
that system has proved the best way of assuring a rising standard of living *with* freedom and liberty. And, so, increasing activity on the part of government seems inevitable in providing
those social measures which are beyond the capacity of any one
industry in a decentralized business system. The "welfare
state" thus turns out to be inextricably entwined with a vigorous science and an aggressive business economy.

Perhaps, if we did not give this trend in government a name
such as "welfare state"—or, even worse, "creeping socialism"—
we would be able to look at reality with truer vision. If demagogues have made business a scapegoat, business has made government the arch villian of the modern world. Business has
assumed all too often over the course of history the role of an
all-out opponent, rather than a friendly critic, of social legislation and kindred measures. Businessmen are prone to forget
that our power systems—business, science, government, morality—are interrelated and inseparable, that together, and only

together, can they nourish and sustain our American civilization in its material, as well as in its moral, strength.

As we finish this story, it becomes clear that the moral dilemma which faces us as Americans is not a burden but rather a privilege. The dilemma—the privilege—is intrinsic in the very structure of our nation as it was conceived by our Founding Fathers in 1776: how to mobilize, tame, and direct power so as to achieve freedom, strength, and human progress. The freedoms we have won and safeguarded, the progress we have made in the abolition of poverty and in the conquest of disease, the industrial and military strength we have mobilized twice during the twentieth century against tyranny, the vision we have shown in recent years in standing by with aid and hope to a shattered world—all these are but dramatic and outstanding chapters in the history of an accountability we have been giving on the use of power before the decent opinion of mankind. To be sure, we have made errors; we have been at times tardy in mobilizing our power in the cause of justice. Nevertheless, as we look back we may feel confident—instead of defensive or fearful—that we shall on the whole give a proper accounting in the years to come, as we have in the past, in dispelling the ominous shadows overhanging mankind, and in freeing the world for the blessings which the great powers of modern times make available.

About The Authors

Benjamin Selekman has since 1945 been Kirstein Professor of Labor Relations at the Harvard Graduate School of Business Administration. Born in Bethlehem, Pennsylvania, his adult life has been spent in social work and the study of industrial and labor relations, where he has established for himself a national reputation. He is the author of several books in the field, one of the more recent being *Labor Relations and Human Relations*.

His late wife Sylvia worked closely with her husband on most of his projects. *Power and Morality in a Business Society* is a bold and striking extension of theories they have developed in the field of industrial relations and applied to the broader areas of national and international affairs.